Numismatic Criminals

"PCGS stealing and fraud"

by troy joseph

I am writing and publishing this book to expose PCGS coin grading service did in fact steal my nickel and the proof is shown here in this book. There are many other cases with victims of stealing and fraud and unprofessional services by PCGS. And they ARE NOT the best 3rd party grader, they are THE WORST AND MOST DISHONEST !!!! What they did to me was very evil (and others) and they think they are so untouchable !! people need to keep complaining and tell their experiences and try to stop this criminal syndicate !!!! There is no coin police to monitor any coin grading activity, this leaves the opportunity WIDE OPEN for CRIME !! and they've been getting away with it for decades. I noticed many other complaints against Collectors Universe also, major frauds and even a 10 million dollar settlement in one case. These people are flat out SCUMBAGS !!! And GOOD LUCK trying to find out their insurance or bonding company !!!!!!! CRIMINALS !! They wont tell you on the phone and try to find record of it in California gov offices. I tried to file a claim for my stolen nickel and could not, **After I show a few obvious PCGS examples of their CRIMES, then I will show pics of the nickel they stole from me and the piece of shit they sent back to me.**

 I am not a professional writer and this book has not been proof read and edited professionally, so please excuse the format. it is meant to just give my experience with the PCGS criminals and share other experiences I found online, websites such as Yelp, pissed customer, and BBB you can see many complaints. Many instances of coin theft. There is a man named Félix Díaz Artista who lives in Mexico, suffers 100,000 USD loss. PCGS figures this man cant do anything because he lives outside of the U.S. I could not find one lawyer to take my case,in the U.S., I can just imagine the problems mr. Artista had trying to get legal help. These attorneys are just as slimy as the criminal. Either they wanted 2000-2500 retainer, or they would make up stories or talk over me and hang up the phone, which is so obvious they are owned by PCGS. Yes indeed thats what I say that PCGS has a lot of paid off numismatic attorneys. My case is so cut & dry its mind boggling why any lawyer did not take the case on contingency. My email is **antiquefineartt@aol.com** if anyone wants to contact me to ask questions, or we can talk about a class action lawsuit.

, But the fact of the matter is the time is here now to expose their crimes. Do they think they are so powerful they can pay off every lawyer in this country and use intimidation to prevent any lawyer from taking cases from people like me who have a legitimate claim, ? and others like myself that have suffered from their wrongdoings,?, In this book is a true account of my claim that they stole my nickel with the entire case I prepared for court, which unfortunately I could not get a lawyer to take the case. There are many others that have suffered losses by this PCGS ! PCGS claims over and over that they are the best coin grading service, well actually this is a lie because of all the unresolved complaints and the complaints that keep arising from their dishonest services. How can anybody claim to be the best, with such facts of stealing, don't even mention that there has never been a court case that has won in favor of a victim. Well this is a high priority for PCGS, to pay off EVERY numismatic attorney in the country, must cost them a lot of money. One serious attention getter when dealing with these crooks is that they refuse to let you speak to anyone, like at PCGS you can only speak to David Rosenberg and nobody else?? He is the main criminal and all others who listen to his orders are accessories and they know damn well what he is doing, For those of you reading this book not familiar with some of the values of these modern coins let me just say that they far exceed the value of a gold coin. High grade examples going up to 25,000 for Nickels, quarters, dimes, and Lincoln cents !! Yes indeed this is where the vultures swoop in on what they think are unsuspecting customers, and swiping their coins using their criminal methods of trickery and lying, word manipulation, and not giving you any clues to what they are doing with your coins. They delay your order and tell you lies, they are looking for other coins to swap out for your coins and during the process of these delays they are hoping that you will agree to their terms of reconditioning or other bogus con-jobs. It is forbidden for you to speak to a coin grader or a coin reconditioning expert that cannot guarantee any grade to the coin or condition of it after "reconditioning services" ? And these are experts ?

 I have contacted others with similar experiences. So in my case being homeless and impossible to come up with any retainer, I just suffered and suffered even more because the sale of my coins was supposed to give me a step up in life so I could get my own house to live in. But because of this obvious theft of my 1956 Jefferson Nickel with full steps, and the other coins in my submission they totally screwed up, I'm very damaged. I went into a deep depression for months devistated, I'll never trust any "professional" . Professional fucking LIARS AND THIEFS !!! Take a look at their propaganda here,,,,,,,,,,,,,,,,,,,,,,,,,,,,,,,,>>

"PCGS is a division of Collectors Universe which is a publicly traded company. In the 32 years since PCGS's founding, Collectors Universe has graded and authenticated over 68 million items for a combined current value of over $35 billion. The nature of our business is that customers submit their coins and other collectibles to us for authentication and grading services. In this instance, this customer received a PCGS graded coin as a gift". BULLSHIT !!. I dont care if you graded 99 trillion coins !!! you are still a coin thief !!! and spreading false propaganda is your expertise among stealing coins. I wonder how many coins were stolen to build up this business ? How many unsuspecting customers were fleeced of their valuable treasures that PCGS swapped out for lesser grade coins. And keep advertising you're the best but keep getting a vast number of complaints every year because you're so "professional" ? Ha ha ha ha . You people make me so sick, you MOTHER FUCKIN CRIMINALS !! and take a look at this shit,,,,,,,,,,,,,,,,,,,

,(found in a BBB complaint response) "As previously stated, PCGS does not buy or sell coins, thus we would not be able to exchange the coin in question". Really ? NO SHIT

DICK TRACEY !!, your dealer friends sell for you.

 Who the hell do you crooks think you're talking to? Do you think everyone is stupid ??
There's many ways to swap-out a coin, I'm sure David Rosenberg & gang has many coin
dealer friends with an adequate supply of coins, with all the delays gives time to find coins
to exchange for the customer's high grade coins, via>making up stories the conservation
had a certain effect on their coin, etc, etc etc etc etc, just make up any story you can think of
and make it sound technical, and return to me my fucking> "gift" that's weeks late and with
a low grade, or just lose it somewhere and send the customer a beater coin. There's over
1000 senerios of how they steal coins, yeah experts at crime, They have PLENTY of friends
that sell coins for them. They all need to be investigated !!! my 1943 DDO Washington
Quarter, MS condition, and my 1943 RPM steel lincoln cent MS condition they kept for 3
½ weeks !!! for a 5 day express service !!! all the while I complained and complained and
complained. Luckily I had them send them back !! and they were ungraded because all my
complaints, at first they had my 1943 DDO quarter listed as a 1942 ! I had to remind them
numerous times (customer service claimed it was just a typo?) during a weeks time until
they corrected my order to where I could see it online in my submission. Yeah they wanted
that quarter real bad. It's very valuable. And what would have happened if I did not
complain so many times ? I've been on the coin forums and the amount of fraud is
staggering. From artificial toned coins, to nickels graded FS (full steps) when they are not
qualified by no means to receive the "FS" designation. Coins have also been over graded. I
could spend over a year just gathering all the evidence and complaints on PCGS !!!! they do
whatever the fuck they want !! see pics I have a couple examples included in this book. A
nickel "FS" which has contact marks all over the steps, (showing seperation in the lines of
the steps which IS NOT ALLOWED) and a nickel that was cooked, it is artificially toned.
Theres plenty more out there, people on youtube also exposing the overgraded morgans.
Heres one recent video showing some washington quarters over-graded.

"ELUSIVE 1969 Washington Quarter Finally Sees BIG Sale! - MONDAY MARKET
REPORT"
 https://www.youtube.com/watch?v=wwBmQEQrx0w

 How do you grade a coin with planchet marks and nicks on the rim and no luster a 67+ or
68, ?? but when you send in your quarters that are in better condition you get a grade of 64-
65?? come on people that's enough of this bullshit WATCH THIS VIDEO !!!! PCGS
FRAUD !!

"Do Grading Services Market Grade? What Is GradeFlation?
 https://www.youtube.com/watch?v=rzPNrxliUf8

Tired Of Loosing Your Money Grading Coins"? Yeah PCGS employees have plenty of dealer friends and relatives for their outlets. (the buddy system), Probably auction house connections also. And these auction houses never question anything ??? Amazing. I seen so many coins falsley graded and sold at auction and nobody questions anything. Old 1909-S vdb lincoln cent obviously been cleaned and with many contact marks and very poor strike quality gets a MS66 grade. It looked like a beater !! but yet because it's in a PCGS slab that means everything is authentic and genuine,,bla bla bla bla,, YEAH RIGHT !!! HOW DOES AN AUCTION HOUSE SELL A NICKEL THAT'S DESIGNATED "FS" WHEN THE STEPS ARE ALL FUCKED UP ?? HOW CAN THIS HAPPEN ???? HELLO OUT THERE !!!! IS ANYBODY AWAKE ?? this is incredible !! the most blatant fraud right under their noses and yet nothing is said. You look at the nickel pics Lets take a look at some pics of a nickel grades MS 66 FS with a CAC sticker sold at heritage auction. Here's the reference.

Home / All Coins / 2018 June 14 - 17 LB Expo US Coins Signature Auction - Long Beach #1276 / Lot #3425

On the next 3 pages you'll see just ONE example what I am talking about, a "BEATER" nickel, plain as day and the auction sold it anyways?? . On the heritage website you can blow up the picture and see the "full steps", yeah right. There's a few hundred more out there graded by these "PROFESSIONAL RIPP-OFFS" Naturally they would say this is normal die state, or some other BS !! yeah !! nice full steps !!! you'll see a close up of this on the next pages check out this winner,

I want to show a couple examples of PCGS's criminal frauds before we get to my coin.

This nickel found on the video called "what is gradeflation" on youtube

Home / All Coins / 2018 June 14 - 17 LB Expo US Coins Signature Auction - Long Beach #1276 / Lot #3425

You can find it sold on heritage auction and zoom in on the steps

from the PCGS website, read below and here is the reference link:
https://www.pcgs.com/news/tips-from-the-grading-room-part-3

Full Steps (FS) is the designation following the numerical grade of some regular-strike MS60 or higher Jefferson nickels that have at least five separated steps (lines) at the base of Monticello. Any major disturbance or interruption of these steps or lines, whether caused by contact, planchet problems, or another source, will result in the coin's not being designated FS. Only the slightest weakness on any step (line) is allowed for this designation. Some issues are almost never seen with Full Steps and may command a significant premium.

YEAH WE SEE THOSE FULL STEPS ! Lol, PCGS criminals !!
And this coin sold at heritage auction for 1500 $. Why doesnt the auction house
check these coins ? OMG !!!!

Lol ! Next coin !! sold for 21,000 in 2008, then 16,000 in 2011, and it's graded a MS66

2008 December Houston, TX Signature Coin Auction #1118 / Lot #215

https://coins.ha.com/itm/lincoln-cents/1936-1c-doubled-die-obverse-type-one-ms66-red-pcgs/a/1118-215.s
2011 February Long Beach Signature US Coin Auction #1152 / Lot #3141

https://coins.ha.com/itm/lincoln-cents/1936-1c-doubled-die-obverse-type-one-ms66-red-pcgs-fs101/a/1152-3141.s?hdnJumpToLot=1&x=0&y=0

1936 DDO 1C lincoln cent, and just to see I'm not making this stuff up, the 3rd pic I had to transfer from heritage website then add my info to it then take pic with phone because the pic would not transfer to a large enough size.

Imaged by Heritage Auctions, HA.com

Imaged by Heritage Auctions, HA.com

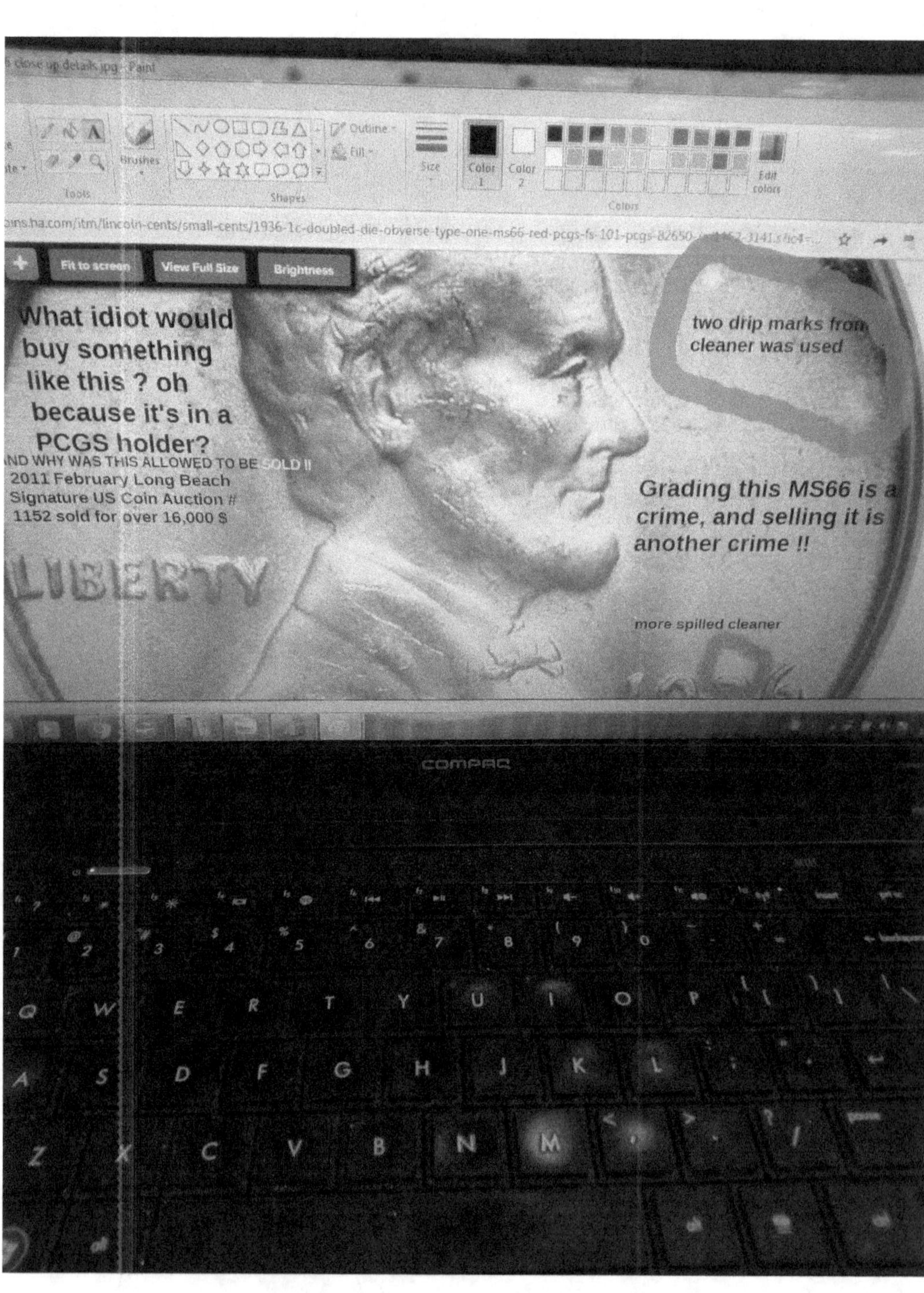

ins.ha.com/itm/lincoln-cents/small-cents/1936-1c-doubled-die-obverse-type-one-ms66-red-pcgs-fs-101-pcgs-82650-ast152-3141.s/io1=
Fit to screen
View Full Size
Brightness
What idiot would buy something like this ? oh because it's in a PCGS holder?
AND WHY WAS THIS ALLOWED TO BE SOLD !!
2011 February Long Beach Signature US Coin Auction # 1152 sold for over 16,000 $
LIBERTY
two drip marks from cleaner was used
Grading this MS66 is a crime, and selling it is another crime !!
more spilled cleaner
COMPAQ

Now we see this beater how it was doctored up with a cleaner and over-graded. I'm not sure what to say about whoever bought this coin, but it has been sold twice, so maybe the first buyer realized it was a fraud and decided to dump it. People should know better, just because it's in a PCGS holder doesn't mean shit !!! there's too much fraud being revealed and I am going to show more examples of PCGS's crimes in my next book, Let me tell you what I see wrong with this 1936 lincoln cent, first of all mr. Jack Lee "pedigree" and being a DDO, and being a 1936, doesn't justify a 66 !! This coin has been rubbed with a cleaner and the idiot that cleaned it spilled 3 drops of cleaner, (PCGS reconditioning expert), there are numerous contact marks also, I also see some black swirly marks in front of the upper ear, looks like possibly some child scribbled this up with a magic marker or ink pen and some of the marks are still visible, the coin really should not have been graded after they (WHOEVER) fucked it up, BUT, like it says on the cover of my book,,,,,,When committing crimes (stealing) is so easy to get away with, why quit? Doctoring up this coin, grading it, and selling are ALL STEALING, ITS CRIMINAL !! you crooks are stealing from the public. And claim youre the best,,, and professionals?? yeah ok buddy.

Here's some comments from the video where I found this 1936 DDO

Frank Truslow1 year ago 100% agree...PCGS is really bad - In fact, I've stopped submitting to PCGS. I could tell some stories.

REPLY Beercan Burr1 year ago

ANACS and NGC should merge, buy PCGS and fire everyone. Just kidding PCGS so please give me a good grade on my Kennedy's that you have.

REPLY rick rosa1 year ago

I agree and have have very hesitate in sending any of my coin's.... Thank's for keeping it real...

REPLY Compton Harsham1 year ago

Daniel, very honest video. THANKS!!! Same questions here. WE NEED TO TAKE THE HUMAN FACTOR OUT OF GRADING AND USE ARTIFICIAL INTELLIGENCE AS SUGGESTED...

REPLY Coin Antics1 year ago You are absolutely right,, I have experienced the exact same thing when having my coins graded..

REPLY Jolene Gallegos1 year ago

I love this video Daneil thank you for helping us know how the grading company's really give their grades...

REPLY

verlon mckay1 year ago Love this video. Opened my eyes WOW People like myself and others that are intelligent enough to catch PCGS in thier dishonesty is not enough to stop them, because like I mentioned before there is no coin police and they will persist with all their dirty deeds because it's so easy to get away with.

 So let's figure on a proportion of numbers out of 75, 000 customers they get 50 complaints. They laugh at that, it's a joke to them. And these are all legitimate complaints of theft by means of swapping coins that are being reconditioned, or just swapping coins that are sent in to be graded, like in my circumstance. They will steal anyway they can. They have the bully lawyer they have the numismatics lawyers paid off, and they keep spreading propaganda about how good they are and how honest they are. As I checked the BBB the complaints are still coming in so PCGS has no intention of quitting their crimes. I just wonder how many thousands-hundreds of thousands, or possibly a million or more of coins PCGS has swapped out or stolen, People like me complaining and others complaining and fighting and fighting for justice and not getting any remedy, they sure do have it figured out how to get away with it, BUT, just imagine how many people assume that PCGS is the most trustworthy coin grader and they do not question anything, people sending in their coins not knowing that they are a high grade MS 66 to MS 68 and are being swapped out and are sent back MS 63 and MS 64's, they agree to the conservation services not knowing that their coins are being swapped out for common blast white coins and telling the customer it is a result from the reconditioning services !! and they take the customers high grade coins and have their buddies sell it for them and they split the money. Yeah they know all the tricks alright, walking liberties, quarters and half dollars with a full head, they're pretty easy to swap out. Mercury times with full bands Roosevelt times with full bands and Jefferson nickels with full steps, and many many other coins. Rare indian head and buffalo nickels can be worth more than gold with certain errors or high grades,

 Especially if you are a newbie first time submitter,, God forbid if you have any beautiful coins cuz they will do anything they can to get their hands on them, just like they did to me. What they didn't know I've looked at thousands and thousands of coins and I've been collecting coins over 8 years and I'm not stupid, That's why I caught them and that's why I have the evidence !!! They also refused to show me any video !! Even though it's supposed to be their policy, fuck the policy right when you have a $9,000 nickel you just stole from somebody, and how many other coins that week that you stole from people. This is the most evilest act somebody is ever done to me, what a dirty mother fucker to steal my coin when I'm trying to work my way up to better myself, I looked at least 1000 nickels to find the best example with full steps, because I wanted NOT to be sleeping in my truck anymore, do you think I would stay up all hours of the night week after week and almost a month looking for the most beautiful nickel for nothing?? (And my other beautiful coins). My eyes are very well trained to pick out the best, this is why people want to steal my coins. PCGS I am convinced is a crime syndicate and the biggest coin thieves in existence.

 They have this very well thought out just like the most complicated murder mystery but this is on a different level of deceit and trickery such as the banks committing mortgage fraud and complicated crimes such as imbezzlement, very similar to bank robbers how a criminal mind must think. They are not after the obvious gold coins or the ancient coins, they seem to be professionals at stealing the coins more valuable, which are high grade examples or rare varieties and errors that they think the first time submitters or the unsuspecting would not question them, or realize their coin had been swapped, they claim to have video surveillance? But when an issue arises that your coin is not the same one that you sent in,,,,,, THERE IS NO VIDEO AND YOU ARE LEFT ARGUING WITH A FUCKING BULLY ATTORNEY !!!! A lot of you out there might be saying you've been using PCGS for so many years and never had a problem, that's what everybody says even with PayPal, but you never had a problem UNTIL IT HAPPENS, but mainly PCGS are experts carefully choosing their victims whether it be first time submitters or whoever they think is inexperienced or ignorant,,,,, whoever they think is not going to pursue them with legal action and they like stealing from women also, But I see many complaints from victims they underestimated,,

I wonder who is the actual masterminds who invents the criteria when they plan to steal a coins or swap them out? I wonder if the CEO knows (joe orlando), how can he not know ? When PCGS gets caught with their dishonest Acts, we the People experience nothing less than rude and arrogant, or very manipulative clever defense attitudes, like they are grasping for a way to weasel out of what they just got caught !! At that point they offer no restitution, no apologies. Of course they're going to say "I'm sorry", well that doesn't mean shit when the customer has suffered a loss !! Sorry doesn't cut it !! So I am the one that has the proof that PCGS is a thief and I can say anything I want because I have the proof of what they did. Like it's some big political public factor that it is forbidden to be known publicly that PCGS has blatantly stole a coin, well it is known now with this book !! We the people can speak up for ourselves because the attorneys are too fucking slimy,,,,, nobody has $2,500 or $4,000 for a retainer which goes right into their pocket as a free gift. These attorneys should be helping people on contingency because most of these cases are so cut and dry it's a no-brainer. Within the next pages you will see my jefferson nickel are the first two pictures, then the following 5 pictures is the nickel they sent back to me, screen shots from Ebay are also included and comparison reference.

Do you really think PCGS is the best coin grader? Anybody can grade millions of coins, just like McDonald's sells millions of hamburgers. PCGS must think a few hundred complaints, or even a thousand complaints is a joke to them, they laugh at it because they have it all figured out over the years !!!! It's nothing to them, they'll just smooth talk their way out of it like on the BBB or pay off whoever. Well there's no smooth talk or excuses for the evidence I am showing, and they picked the wrong customer to F with this time.

well let me tell you something folks we got a big big problem here,
and there needs to be an investigation. Now that there is reasonable suspicion of a crime syndicate with the evidence in my book and I'm talking hardcore evidence and complaints. I can just imagine how many thousands of coins if not a million have not been complained about or known to be stolen. I'm only scratching the surface here with my complaint and about 40 to 50 other complaints. But these are all true & legitimate. Wait till you see the pictures of the nickel that I sent in and the nickel that they sent back to me !! And David Rosenberg tried so hard with his con jobs to get that nickel back and I refused to send it back. **That's why now I have the evidence that proves what I claim. PCGS IS A COIN THIEF !!**

E PLURIBUS UNUM
MONTICELLO
FIVE CENTS
UNITED STATES OF AMERICA

The next 6 pics is the one they sent back to me, And compare this scratched up
MS65 nickel to the MS65 washington quarter at the end of this book. My
beautiful washington quarter they gave the same grade as this nickel

i'll bet I could find 100 coins a week that PCGS has inconsistant or fraudulently
graded if I made a career out of it.

1956
5C
PCGS MS65
4059.65/37904679

HEY PCGS YOU DIRTY THIEF !! I GOT THE EVIDENCE RIGHT HERE !~!

ok folks, now how can PCGS's attorney defend them with such evidence as this ?? and how can other attorneys refuse to take this case after seeing this evidence?? the whole coin grading system smells LIKE SHIT !!
 ALL CORRUPT, Im leaving ANACS and ICG out of this, its PCGS AND NGC thats the criminals, wait till you see my evidence I have on NGC what they did to me.

ONTICELL

Comparison nickel (to mine), sold for 9400.00

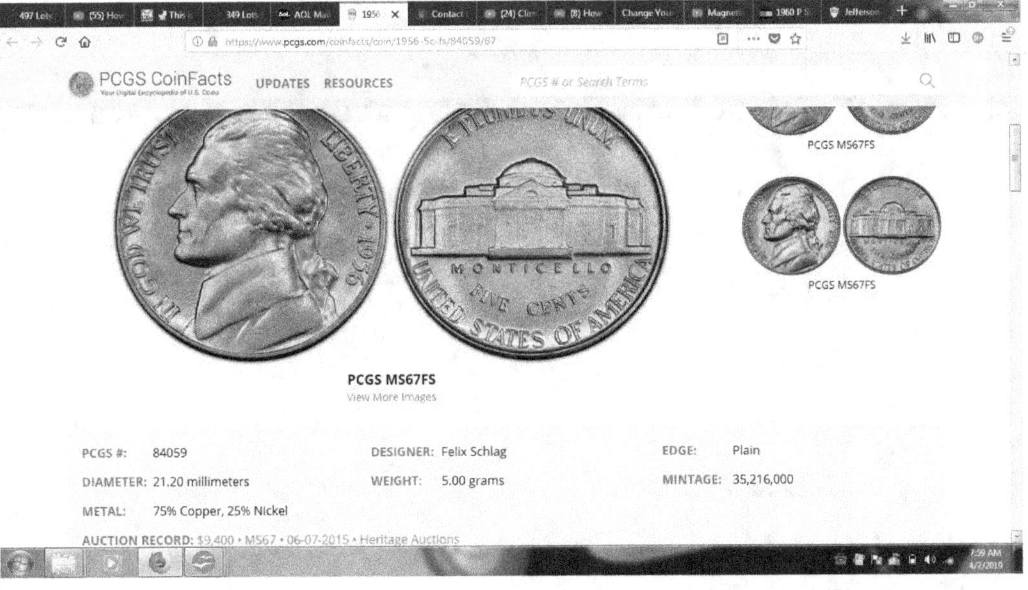

There's my nickel I purchased from Ebay, I removed my address in case anybody gets any ideas.

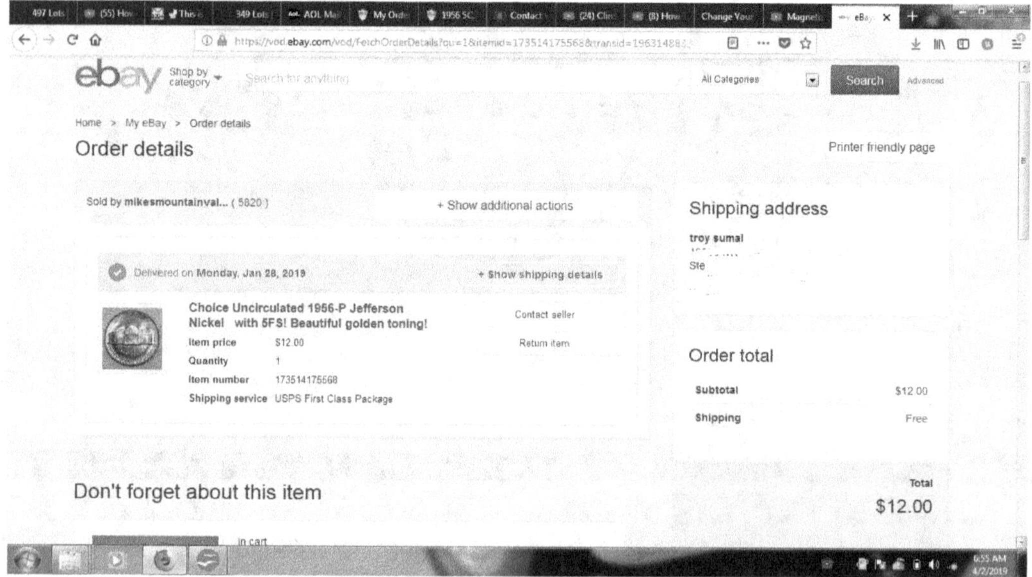

Yeah folks it doesn't matter who you are or what you claim to be or what you claim your reputation is, there are thieves and liars rampant in this world and that's just the way it is, the biggest thieves from my experience are the ones that claim to be the most professional and the most successful. Look at Wells Fargo and Bank of America how much criminal fraud felonies they have on their records, judges,
police, chain stores, food stores, hotels motels, restaurants, car dealers, any type of business you can imagine just research it and I guarantee you're going to see bad reports of fraud and stealing, just because PCGS claims to be the biggest and the best coin grader **doesn't mean it is so**, there are thieves working within this company which think they are so clever nobody can catch them !! keep claiming how many coins you graded, like what does that mean ??

, But the fact of the matter is the time is here now to expose their crimes. Do they think they are so powerful they can pay off every lawyer in this country and use intimidation to prevent any lawyer from taking cases from people like me who have a legitimate claim, ? and others like myself that have suffered from their wrongdoings,?, In this book is a true account of my claim that they stole my nickel with the entire case I prepared for court, which unfortunately I could not get a lawyer to take the case. There are many others that have suffered losses by this PCGS ! With the amount of evidence I have no lawyer (law-liar) would respond from legalmatch online.

PCGS claims over and over that they are the best coin grading service, well actually this is a lie because of all the unresolved complaints and the complaints that keep arising from their dishonest services. How can anybody claim to be the best, with such facts of stealing, don't even mention that there has never been a court case that has won in favor of a victim. Well this is a high priority for PCGS, to pay off EVERY numismatic attorney in the country, must cost them a lot of money. I found out their yearly net profits was 56 million avg per year. That leaves plenty of $$$ for pay-offs !!! They can just steal a million $$ worth of coins to pay their (bribery budget), Theyre dam good at stealing, they been getting away with it for all these years.

One serious attention getter when dealing with these crooks is that they refuse to let you speak to anyone, like at PCGS you can only speak to David Rosenberg and nobody else?? He is the main criminal and all others who listen to his orders are accessories and they know damn well what he is doing, For those of you reading this book not familiar with some of the values of these modern coins let me just say that they far exceed the value of a gold coin. High grade examples going up to 25,000 for Nickels, quarters, dimes, and Lincoln cents !! Yes indeed this is where the vultures swoop in on what they think are unsuspecting customers trying to swipe their coins using their criminal methods of trickery and lying, word manipulation, and not giving you any clues to what they are doing with your coins. When they delay your order and tell you lies, they are looking for other coins to swap out for your coins and during the process of these delays they are hoping that you will agree to their terms of reconditioning or other bogus con-jobs. It is forbidden for you to speak to a coin grader or a coin reconditioning expert that cannot guarantee any grade to the coin or condition of it after "reconditioning services" ? And these are experts ? They think that you think it's just a quarter, and they are hoping that you just agree to let them do whatever they want because they claim to be such an expert and of course it's on Google anyways isn't it ? And when you disagree and go against the grain then the problems begin. They delay your order, and or swap out the coins anyway during reconditioning, or screw up your coins, or send them back ungraded. They might keep your perfect examples and they send you back damaged coins or other coins at a lower grade !!! There is no board of directors to speak to no CEO nobody higher up in the chain of command, just one criminal (david rosenberg), who evidently has control over the most part of the crime syndicate. He thinks he is so smart that nobody will ever come after him for his crimes, he is a highly experienced smooth talkin TRIXTER/DECIEVER, well trained to fool most customers. He writes so polite and smooth in such a way to gain confidence of the BBB. But people like me will expose his miscreant acts, and I dont give up. Im anxious to see his response on my new BBB complaint !!

It amazes me that this keep going on year after year with complaints, their CEO and board of directors dont seem to have any concern for these re-occuring incidents of theft and fraud. This is why I can conclude that there's so much $$$$$$$$ to be made and NO investigations, no arrests !!! they will just continue their crimes. If there is any court cases, they'll just settle out of court, no big deal. They're still laughing at everyone !!!

From reviewing the complaints on pissed customer and Yelp it would seem that they are targeting new submissions from people that they think are amateurs, I wonder how many coins they have actually stolen that the customer is not even aware of. Reconditioning the coins is a great smoke screen to swap out coins and get away with the stealing. They can make up any reason they want and from what I have read on the complaints there is no guarantee for their reconditioning services?? and these are professionals ??

Not only did they steal my valuable nickel, I have every reason to believe they tried to steal two other coins which were delayed by three weeks for no reason whatsoever, I have every reasonable suspicion to believe they were trying to find replacement coins to swap out for my 1943 BU DDO Washington quarter, and my 1943 steel Lincoln cent RPM , they got pissed off of all my complaining about what is going on with these two coins for 3 weeks ungraded and then they sent them back to me raw!;!!!, This is not a professional coin grading service this is just some crooked ass motherfuckers with a thug for an attorney, keep in mind these high grade modern coins and these double die error coins are more valuable than gold !!! they also like to rip off the women coin collectors I see, So PCGS can keep up all their propaganda about how they are the best but on the other side where there is truth we see all the complaints on the websites and we can just estimate how many people just give up and dont do anything,,,,,,,,, and some where the customer isn't even aware of what they're doing !! A lot of you out there might be saying you've been using PCGS for so many years and never had a problem, that's what everybody says about paypal until their account gets frozen for no reason, but you never had a problem UNTIL IT HAPPENS, but mainly PCGS's experts carefully choose their victims whether it be first time submitters or whoever they think is inexperienced or vunerable, whoever they think is not going to pursue them with complaints and legal action, (well they have a bully lawyer to deal with anyways which is extremely arrogant and on a power trip), and they like stealing from women also, I wonder who is the actual masterminds who make up the criteria and orchestrate the plan when they plan to steal a coins or swap them out. I know David Rosenberg is one of them for sure,,And I wonder how customer service deals with all the complaining customers and yet still choose to work for crooks, they should know by now PCGS is a criminal, maybe theyre getting a kick-back ? I wouldn't doubt it. AND HERE'S ANOTHER CASE I FOUND, !!

5000.00 $ COIN STOLEN Victor H. Alhambra, WOW,, WHAT A RIP-OFF !!
CA 64 friends 125 reviews 55 photos
Share review Embed review
7/3/2019 Updated review
Here I am again!!!@!#! Years later at the Long Beach Coin Expo. At the Long Beach Convention Center. And guess what I thought I would do ---??? I went back to PCGS to risk them reviewing my 1909-s MS65Indian Cent, that is in their own (older) green holder. I wanted them to re-examine the coin for possible upgrade, and take pictures and reholder it in their new coin slabs. How difficult is that!... I paid $103.00 for them to reconsider the grade and at the very least, put the coin in a new holder with their photo and Gold shield service~~~ What I received ~~~ a blue plastic coin box with the coin in its' original coin holder (old green slab), and the submittal paperwork!.... Nothing was done! No new holder, no photos....NOTHING! That's all they did at their facility in Huntington Beach, they looked at it, or it in a box, and sent it back!!!! $103.00 later ---!!!! .... So I called their Customer Service and explained what I received. I asked if there was something that the agent Joanne missed on the form to have the coin in a new slab and photographed?... She said that "All you need to do was write in the coin description area that you want both. We will send you a return order at no expense to you, and we will re-holder and photograph the coin for you.". [Why didn't Joanne, at the Long Beach Coin Show, do that to begin

with!!???] , I made myself clear about what I wanted at least three times while filling out my information on the Coin Submittal Form. And she assured me that all that would be done.... Customer Service on the phone, said they would send me a return (RMA), and when they received the coin back again, they would re-holder it and photograph it with gold shield....no charge to me. For that, I added a star~~~ I'll post again when I receive the final product... I won't get my hopes up much... It's Been two weeks ---- I've been waiting for my promised RMA label to send the 1909-S Indian Cent back to PCGS for reslabbing with the new gold shield and their high end photos.... What did I get so far..??? ~~~~ NOTHING! No letter, no label, no phone call...no Anything!!!@@!! ... Why should that NOT surprise me. After all, it is PCGS with their noses wayyyyy up in the air (I should offer them Kleenex to wipe the blood coming out of their noses from the high altitude---lol). So do I risk calling them to send me the RMA and have them get their ruddy hands on my $5,000.00+ coin????? What could they possibly do to hose that up!??? Any thoughts folks?~~~ Out.

ANOTHER COMPLAINT !!

10/29/2013Previous review
 Lately, I had someone else send in a few coins for me to PCGS and guess what! ? The cheep coins were graded appropriately and the more expensive expensive ones were graded as CLEANED!.....Hummmm? Is it because I don't go through a coin dealer that has a financial relationship with them PCGS and cost more to go through them... and private citizens that submit their coins as individuals are beat up by the PCGS's graders. ..? Kind of like representing yourself in court without an attorney! ?!.... Judges are always more strict on those that represent themselves----because after all. ..they were once attorneys at one time and that's how they make a living! ....hummmmm?

AND ANOTHER,,,,,,,,,,,,,,

 Ben W. Los Angeles, CA
 0 friends 17 reviews
 Share review Embed review 10/9/2020
 PCGS graded three of my grandmother's coins. They were shipped to me via UPS and UPS lost them. UPS investigated it and found the loss claimable, and sent PCGS the claims paperwork. That was on August 27th. I've have called six to eight times since August 27th (it's now October 9th) and no one has called me back to give me the status of my claim. Keep in mind, UPS is simply waiting on them to file the paperwork so that I can get my money back from my coins. PCGS is sitting on several hundred dollars of my money and no one will tell me what the status of that is.

AND ANOTHER,,,,,,,,,,,,,,,,,,,,

 P. S. Los Angeles, CA
 0 friends 15 reviews
 Share review Embed review 11/22/2019 Updated review Update:
 This "counterfeit" coin sold at UK auction for £3,500 (roughly $4,500 USD) recently. F**k you, PCGS. Useful 3 Funny 2 Cool 1 6/12/2019Previous review

 A total joke of a company, don't waste your time with these amateurs. My father has been a UK based metal detectorist for over 40 years. He sent them a one-of-a-kind, almost perfect condition silver Anglo Saxon penny (which he retrieved from farmland). He was interested in selling it on the US market, and needed authentication. PCGS didn't slab the coin, they just took one look and deemed it counterfeit (probably because it was cleaned). LAUGHABLE! Thanks for having us waste $200 (after shipping and fees) on your pathetic service. The coin has since been deemed genuine by a UK authenticator, and will sell there.

Complaints from BBB with my comments added in red type

24 Complaints on The BBB website Show All Complaints • Sort By Most Recent • Complaint Type: Problems with Product/Service Status:

Answered 10/04/2020
I sent in two orders to have coins graded under the "Summer 50" special. The first one only had 6 coins on it to grade; So, I sent in another one with 10 coins so that they could be processed with the first. The 16 coins together meet the 10 or more coins required for the free shipping special. I called customer service and talked to Paulina at 12:20 PM who told me that they could not be combined because they were on separate order forms. All 16 coins are in grading and none have been shipped out yet. I was charged an extra $27.00 I did not authorize on my credit card for the service. I want this amount credited back to me. You should be able to ship the two orders together under the special without any problem.

J Response 10/15/2020
Hello. I apologize for the delay in responding. PCGS does not offer combined shipping to customers who have multiple orders being processed. Each order is processed individually and each order is completed individually. Once an order is completed, it is shipped back to the customer. PCGS has thousands of customers, many who have multiple orders at various stages of the grading and authentication process. Each order is shipped back to the customer individually once the order is completed.

Customer Response 10/15/2020
There were two problems: PCGS did not honor their free shipping agreement and they charged an extra $27 to my credit card without authorization.

J Response 10/22/2020 As noted in our previous reply, PCGS processes thousands of orders and orders are shipped when they are completed. The option to "combine shipping" across multiple orders is not something that PCGS can accommodate and accordingly this customer was notified of that fact. For the order of 10 coins, the customer received free shipping as part of the offered promotion. For the order of less than 10 coins, the customer was charged for shipping based o For the order of 10 coins, the customer received free shipping as part of the offered promotion. For the order of less than 10 coins, the customer was charged for shipping based on the terms and conditions listed on the submission form that the customer signed. As part of the terms and conditions, the customer agrees that any shipping, handling, or grading fees will be automatically updated if necessary. While I apologize for the confusion, this customer was notified that combined shipping is not possible (for both logistical and insurance reasons) and did agree to the terms as stated on the forms. If this customer would like to reach out to me directly, I am happy to work with them on coming up with an amicable solution.' Thank you. David R******** dr********@collectors.com

Complaint Type: Problems with Product/Service Status:

Answered 08/11/2020

So I sent in some coins to be graded by PCGS. 5 total. 2 came back encapsulated and graded and 2 were counterfeit and one was not attempted due to no date elegiblaty.I didn't write down a date because I choose to have it "mint error" service. So they didn't even attempt to mint grade it. A dime they claimed was counterfeit manade error had a clear date of 2015 or 2005 on it. Clear plantchet error. I weighed it on a digital scale and matched those of the years listed so I sent it in.I figure it should have been a "error planchet coin".This is were it gets tougher. THE 60' D nickle was kinted at 64 but I felt they didn't research it good enoughf. Simply eye balled it to mint. On the picture images you can clearly see errors on the reverse (AMERICA and MONTICELLO). The structure too. Clear dubble die error from printing. If you zoom in on their pictures you can make the errors out.Front as well.The 1976 1976 D drummer boy 25 cent quarter came back at AU55. But also forgot the "Double Die Error" on the front Washington's face. On the images witch I paid 5$ extra per coin shows plantchet error of the "NOSE, CHIN, And MOUTH". They clearly didn't label my coins correctly and inspected them(reaserch). There are videos only on coin auctions with similar coins being sold. What's the deal?? Looks like I got scammed.

 M Response 08/12/2020 We have reviewed the customer's complaint as well as the transcript from Mr. *****' call to our customer service department on August 5, 2020. PCGS' customers pay us to validate the authenticity and evaluate the quality of coins and banknotes. We use consensus grading with multiple graders looking at each item and Mr *****' coins were reviewed and authenticated in this fashion. We stand behind our evaluation of the customer's coins, with 2 of the 5 coins deemed authentic and receiving a grade, 2 of the 5 coins deemed counterfeit because they had been altered, and a fifth coin that we were unable to determine a date and can't verify authenticity due to the condition and, as such, we did not charge the customer for an evaluation of this coin. Unfortunately, sometime we have to tell customers the coins they thought were valuable, aren't. In this case, 2 of the coins Mr. ***** submitted were made to look like errors printed at the Mint, but upon inspection, it was determined that the errors were man-made, meant to look like Mint Errors. While we can appreciate that this result is a disappointment to the customer, it is the job that we are paid to do.

Customer Response 08/12/2020
 So how does one an authentic approval from n those "called blank planchets,and foreign coin US planchets". Like those examples shown on the auction shows. On the internet for sale with authentic labels and scan codes for transfers. WHY DIDNT ANYONE CATCH MY DOUBLE DIE ERROS ON MY 2 AUTHENTIC COINS.? I used 5x, 10x, 15x, and took it to 30x. To insure it was what I was looking at. Like for example your PCGS graded coin at (Collector s Alliance Inc) Golden Dollar Blank Error - PCGS Certified Product Code: 20799 Our Price: $69.95. WHAT ABOUT HOW THEY MAKE AND GRADE THOSE WITH LIGHT SCRATCHES MADE AND POINTED OUT ON THE ACTION VIDEOS TO SELL AS ERRORS. Who's do grade older coins.? Another example. You didn't do your job at all. Proof in hand.
****
****
****
****
****
************* **

 M Response 08/19/2020
 The customer's follow up questions are difficult to decipher but I believe Mr. ***** is asking about the 2 coins there were graded by PCGS, wondering why they were not identified and labeled as "Mint Errors". In speaking with our grading team about the coins in question, here is what I have discovered. Our graders were correct not to designate these items as mint errors. The minor doubling on the reverse of the 1960 Jefferson is not a Fivaz-

Stanton listed variety, and thus not one we recognize. Countless extremely minor varieties such as this exist. As for the second coin in question, the effect the customer is describing on the obverse of the bicentennial quarter is the result of excessive die erosion and is neither a mint error nor a recognized variety. As mentioned in our previous response, unfortunately sometime we have to tell customers the coins they thought were valuable or rare or an error variety, aren't. While we can appreciate that this result is a disappointment to the customer, it is the job that we are paid to do.

Complaint Type: Problems with Product/Service Status: Resolved 03/27/2020 *resolved ?? really ?? BBB always claims resolved from bullshit responses from criminals !!!just because sombody "responds", doesnt mean that "response" is VALID !!*

PCGS Coin Grading Service //Collectors// stole my rare coin,and replaced it with another coin. This 1942/1 coin is worth $73,000-$120,000 dollars. I sent my 1942/1 mercury dime after taking pictures of it ,i compared it that looked the same as my coin but did not look as rare as my coin.I paid a grading fee of $65.00 grading, and shipping/handling fee of 46.00 I mailed my coin to PCGS on (03-03-2020), PCGS received it on (03-09-2020). After veiwing the cpin with my microscope it sowed that the coin had been swapped/ stolen , the coin received by me is graded (AU 58), my coin should be graded (ms 66 - 67) . I called " PCGS" on (03-24-2020) , and talked to a Ms. Paulina C*****, and informed her that the coin i received from "PCGS" was not my coin i forwarded for grading, she seemed surprised when i asked her for the names of who received the coin when it arrived at (PCGS) , and who graded the (AU 58), Ms. Paulina C***** stated that she could not give me that kind of information. Ms. Paulina C***** asked me to send her pictures of the coin i received from (PCGS) , and pictures of my coin submitted to (PCGS) , which i did on (03-24-2020) . I, have yet to get an response from (PCGS) concerning this matter of someone swapping my coin and sending a different coin to me. Before ending my conversation with Ms. Paulina, I asked her why do i need to send pictures of the swapped thats in their " Clear view data base, which i paid a fee of $5.00 for that service. She stated that clear view pictures are very murky and do not show a clear pictures. I can`t understand why i can view the coin on clear view , and no one at PCGS can`t seeba clear view of the coin i paid $5.00 for. I, am going to pursue major legal actions, as i have proof of my real coin, PCGS cannot do the same thing. I want my refund of over $111.00 , and i want my rare or,at least an replacement of equal value .

F Response 03/27/2020
This complaint is the first contact that I have had with this customer and I am engaging him directly to try and resolve the issue. *Over the past thirty-five years PCGS **has graded and authenticated over 43 million coins.*** REALLY ? WHO GIVES A FUCK !!! THAT DOESNT MAKE A DEFENCE FOR STEALING !!
\As part of a public company, PCGS maintains strict processes and controls to ensure that the coins a customer sends in are the same coins that the customer receives back. These controls are tested on a regular basis by an independent third-party. Additionally, PCGS does not maintain an inventory of coins from which a coin could be accidentally switched. *How can a coin be accidentally switched? It might have been an accident? It seems PCGS has many of these accidents !!* From the time each package is opened until the time items are returned to the customer, the complete process is done under camera to protect both customers and employees. *Really ?? where is our videos that we ask for ??* To be quite frank, it is almost impossible *"almost impossible" but when PCGS with all their dealer friends it is QUITE PROBABLE TO SWITCH OUT A COIN !!* for a coin to be switched out with another coin of the exact same date/denomination. I will continue to work with the customer directly to try and resolve this issue and provide him confidence that the coin he received back is in fact the same coin that was sent in.
David R******** - VP, Operations Customer Response 03/27/2020

Better Business Bureau:
I have reviewed the response made by the business in reference to complaint ID 14248602, and find that this

resolution would be satisfactory to me. I will wait for the business to perform this action and, if it does, will consider this complaint resolved.Regards, Frederick J****** *Oh so the BBB is a coin expert now ?? why isnt the department of justice investigating all these complaints ?? or the ANA??*

Complaint Type: Billing/Collection Issues Status:
Answered 10/08/2019
I paid $57 to insure 8 coins which I sent to PCGS because I thought they may be worth over $18,000. These coins graded low and I do not think they are now worth $300. PCGS still charged my debit card $57 to return them to me. The Postmaster studied the box and tracking # in detail. PCGS did not spend over $17 to return them to me, and they were insured for $50 only. I have called PCGS and they say that that was written in the contract I signed when I submitted the coins. After being on hold a while, I was told that PCGS had privately insured these coins for over $18,000. I do not believe that. What if my coins had been lost? PCGS obviously knows the values of my coins ($300?) and I never would have received over $18,000 from PCGS. PCGS grades coins. I don't care if it's in the contract, this is this not the correct way to run their business. They owe me at least $40. Almost everybody gets their coins back from PCGS graded lower than expected. Just go to YouTube, people make videos of opening their returned graded coins from PCGS. Think of all the people they have overcharged for return insurance? What good is this supposedly private insurance which I paid for? I don't believe it exists. PCGS makes enough money from us coin collectors. I see I can write more. I paid PCGS $250 for a membership but became ill and was given 1 year to try to submit my coins. I was still ill a year later. So I wrote them many emails asking for more time to submit the coins. I have all those emails to PCGS, and I never received a reply. I did not call because the first woman I spoke to at PCGS ever was just so nasty! $250 down the drain. Then they automatically took another $250 out of my checking account. Yes, I know it's automatic. So, I've spent $500 plus 2 payments of $57 for shipping, and I have coins worth about $300.

E Response 10/16/2019

Unfortunately PCGS does sometime have the difficult job of telling a customer that the coins they thought were worth a significant amount of money are actually worth less than the customer anticipated. It is for this reason that PCGS offers Price Guides, Auction Prices Realized, Photograde, and other numismatic information online so that customers can make an informed decision about the potential value of their submissions. We also have a vast PCGS Authorized Dealer network to help customers identify coins that can have significant value add by third-party grading. When coins are submitted to PCGS, they are analyzed by multiple experts to determine authenticity and grade (regardless of value). With regard to return shipping, PCGS purchases outside insurance through multiple insurers that are backed by international underwriters. The USPS/FedEx label on the package does not include the insurance costs as purchased through these third-party insurers. Customers can rest assured that all packages shipped by PCGS are insured at the declared value as listed by the customer on their original submission form. Due to this customer's bad experience, I would be happy to work with them personally on future submissions to help streamline the process. Thank you

Customer Response 10/16/2019

PCGS knew my coins were not worth over $18,000. Why did they insure them for that amount with a 3rd party insurer? I paid $57 for exactly what? The real shipping was less than $17 as I was told by the Postmaster. If those coins were lost I never would have received over $18,000. They must do this same thing to everyone. I am owed $40.

Complaint Type: Problems with Product/Service Status: Answered 02/14/2019

I joined this company back in December as a gold member and paid $149. This company it's supposed to be the top grading coin service there is. There is others. In order to sell your coins at auction Heritage / Sotheby's you have to have them graded professionally and encased in a holder with a grade before you can even auction them off I got an inherited some incredible beautiful coins over a hundred years old some very old. I sent these coins in. In December I requested a membership and in January I received a packet that was incomplete 12 Days Later I get the paperwork that should have been in my packet that I paid for I sent my coins in I'm not complaining about the grading. Which did not look like any of their example grading pictures they have online I'm complaining about the customer service no contact no replies zero.I finally got my stuff back my coins 15 1st time 13 last time. 28 total coins. **I've come to find out theft has occurred the old game of switch I have contacted my state BBB in Washington state.Orange County District Attorney's office has contacted me. Since this happened through the postal service is now considered Federal but I still wanted to file this complaint.I have never filed a complaint before against any business but this is family heirlooms that were given to me and very valuable - that were stolen. It's bad customer service no replies, my billing I paid for a service that I didn't get I have no control whatsoever over my credit card and how they bill me,, they bill me as they want and now in the process I'm dealing with theft BBB in Washington state told me that there were over 10 complaints against this company and they are the ones that gave me the phone number to Orange County District Attorney's office I have not filed a case report yet with the police because I'm following protocol. The District Attorney's office did contact me. It has become fedral.** Contacting my post inspectors in my area and file the paperwork.

 B Response 02/21/2019 PCGS processes more than 2,000,000 coins a year. In our 33 years of operating, PCGS has multiple and extensive procedures in place to ensure that each coin submitted is the exact coin returned to the customer. We are 100% confident that the coins returned to Brad were the ones originally submitted by him. As to his complaint about his credit card charges, he was charged the correct fees. His original submission form, that he completed and signed, does have the total amount due for the submissions. PCGS did need to process this over two separate charges, however the total he provided and authorized, is correct.

 Customer Response 02/21/2019 It doesn't surprise me that PCGS what promote their million of coins and s and they're awesome security here's one of my examples **Well if you're the customer service manager David why haven't you replied to my eight emails ? Why haven't you replied about my switched coins. 2 orders 18 out of 28. Very gutsy move Very good pictures were taken. it's only obvious. And I'm not finished with that. My billing inquiries my grading complaints. Questions. A gold membership package that was incomplete I categorized my specimens the way I felt they were valued not the way you guys feel and what you think it should be..because you couldn't get my order done in time Its called a submission form. Called declared value. Postal Service said you picked up my package from January 26th at 7:51 a.m. but 6 days later pcgs sent me an email statement my package showed it arrived that day. Thats Called a lie.** *Thats what they do is DELAY the order to locate coins for swapping out!!* Express means Express just because you couldn't get it finished doesn't mean you can re categorize my order,. keep it as long as you want switch my specimens. I'm on to that. At the end of my membership dont not recharge my credit card. this is your notice. Sent from Yahoo Mail on Android On Tue, Feb 12, 2019 at 4:08 PM,

 David **** <*****@collectors.com> wrote: Good Afternoon Bradley, My name is David ****, I am the Customer Service Manager for PCGS, our Photography team alerted me to your order and you checking to see why this order was processed as Economy versus Express as you submitted it under the Express Service Level. I was able to confirm with our Grading Room Manager that the order was processed as Economy instead of as Express as the market value of the coins on this submission form were closer to the Economy Service Level than the Express Service Level. *The man paid for express service but PCGS needed more time to find coins to swap-out for his. They do what they want, they speak politely to attempt to cover up their criminal acts.* As a courtesy, we processed the order as Economy but in the turnaround time for Express, *what the hell does this mean ?? OMG they ripped this guy off so bad !!* we also imaged each coin as the coins would have been imaged through the

Express Service Level anyways.

Customer Response 02/25/2019

 I have now sent three messages. To the Inspector General Postal Service. It's apparent the process has failed. It's apparent to me that in today's life No 1 Teaches process anymore. This is why we're having problems in general Society I have filled out their paperwork I have sent three inquiries. It doesn't surprise me. Lazy workers. Companies like PCGS continue to thrive on the public and operate. **They just settle out of court I spent many hours over the weekend reading up on their lawsuits and their complaints that sound so similar to mine. I'm no stranger to it now PCGS will continue to function because the process doesn't work I'm proof of it. I will cut my losses and at 55 years old still learn how evil thieves people can be..** advertising that you are Coin Grading service but all along you use a computer that scans and gives you a number on that coin. Grading coins somebody has to program and put a script in this box which they only have access to. There is no security that's how you do 2 million coins a year you use a machine, and that's not what I paid for / and that's not what they're advertising. From day one to an incomplete packet on my membership bad company service doesn't follow their own paperwork. **There process, so they can steals and replaces your items**. Very well known in the past / from lawsuits but I guess for another $425 they get a good rating I'm done with this. Its a joke. Scam...... using a machine to grade your coins when you advertise the Sheldon standard of Coin Grading. But don't tell anybody you're using the computer to grade your Specimen instead of a human. I bet if they put that in their advertisement the company would go broke. It's misleading and a lie. Apparently the inspector-general must be on vacation.. this is the worst experience I've ever had stuff like this never happen 25 years ago B U T It does now - doesn't it.

 B Response 02/27/2019

We are 100% confident that the coins returned to Brad were the ones originally submitted by him. *Thats exactly what david rosenberg wrote to me,,,, he is 100% confident, bet we SEE THE EVIDENCE IN THIS BOOK, this "david rosenberg is 100% fuckin liar"!!* Brad purchased a membership on 12/21/18. I believe his complaint of an incomplete package was due to submission forms not being included however during the last weeks of 2018, our sub forms were expiring, we had not yet received the 2019 sub forms. In order to not delay his and other customers membership kits, these were shipped without sub forms. The submission forms are available on our website and were finally shipped to Brad on 1/8. Brad has submitted 2 orders in the last 2 months. Submission 5818135 was sent first, it was in process with PCGS 1/17-1/28/19, for 15 coins. This submission was sent for Express Service, but he requested to use his free voucher (included with his Gold Membership) as partial payment. Brad was contacted by email explaining that the voucher was not available to use for Express Service ($65/coin), the order would need to be processed under Regular ($35/coin), Brad approved this change. His charge for this order was changed from $847, which he calculated on his sub form, to the approved $442 actual charge to his credit card. Brad's second submission ******* was submitted for Express ($65/coin), he submitted 13 coins. During the processing of the submission, our Operations team realized that these coins were being submitted for a higher service (Express), but were low value coins. They decided that instead of charging the customer $65/coin, which would be a high overpayment vs the actual value of the coins, the fee and service tier were changed to Economy ($27/coin). This was done simply to save out customer some money. By changing the service tier, this did not change the actual outcome of the grading or the turnaround time. The fees charged for this submission was $427, instead of the $986 that the customer submitted for. This submission was still completed in 6 bus days, Express service has an estimated turnaround time of 5 bus days

Customer Response

02/28/2019 Stephanie

My 2000p SAC A roll I had for19 yrs in my safe.Switched with a ugly one ms67.Not mine 2nd.An1999 Connecticut p 25c was in the package replaced black wear on it.Took great picture I can prove it.3rd 1976 25c clad.Bicentennial the drummer had a full rim it was beautiful replaced.Not full rim.Have pictures.4th 1999 Delaware 25c p switched replaced with junk. Submission# *******.My 5th item my 2nd Sac dollar same roll perfect.Switched with a big scratch on the four head.Doesn't match my pictures MS66.#6 2006 d 25c north Dakota MS65 not mine.I took Incredible close up pictures non argumentable.7th 2006 p 5 c. Monticello FS it was a beautiful apricot.Switched.#8th. 2004 d 5c peace medal.Gave me MS64 not even mine. No mach again.9th 1967 50c AU53.Toned yellow.It has red dots on it my picture doesn't.Switched again.Replaced with junk.#10 2004 d 5 c keel boat.Switched does not match same..Junk-MS64.#11 1961d 5 c D/D rare.Monticelli last sold 22k.Pcgs dem it damage and killed it off.It.PCGs your company has a history of this,very thing and lawsuits pending today.For theift switching and damage.Question if you're a Coin Grading service and you admitted you graded over 2 mil. Sheldon grading system? You should not be using a lazor scanner with a script.how else could you pump out 2 mil coins a year does your customers know you're using a lazor scanner for grading.Do they? Question how many coins get lasered. From that machine patent numberis on file Also my order from the post office.Confirmed that my order was picked up on Jan 26th at 7:51am in house that day.But 6 days later,I got my email state's your orders arrived. Lie.I sent an email asking where it was.6 days later. Great security long enough to do whatever you wanted to my order. *They were finding coins to swap-out for yours,,like they do to everybody !!* Postal service is lying to me.? My appt with the inspector general is forthcoming.**Swiching steeling and changing the submission,,6 days unaccounted.Its theft and then down graded my submission form to justifie the theif**.

Complaint Type: Problems with Product/Service

Status: Answered 12/21/2018

 On Nov.15, 2018 i submitted a packet to PCGS for coin grading services. Days later , the company submitted a photo of coin: 1958 Franklin Half dollar appeared on my member web page. **This was not my coin. After talking to a PCGS representive they said my coin. To resolve the matter, I asked to inspaect the photos and videos of the examination process concerning coin only. This was denied. They also stated they are refusing my FOIA request.** The company has misplace my coin.

Customer Response 12/31/2018

 Good Day to All. My original complaint regarding my missing coin is this. The .company PCGS has received my request to inspect the records, photos and video contact not my submission, which in turn will identify my coin (1958 Franklin Half Dollar). This will provide proof of assertion that my coin has been lost by PCGS. Sincerely, Leslie ******* L

Response 01/07/2019
*PCGS processes more then 2,000,000 coins a year. *same ole broken record here, doesnt mean a dam thing*
We have multiple processes and procedures in place to ensure that each coin submitted is the exact coin returned to the correct customer who submitted it. For security reasons, we are not able to release photos or videos from inside of our secure processing facility, however we are 100% confident after a thorough investigation that the coin that was submitted to PCGS by Leslie ***** was the coin returned to Leslie *****

. Customer Response 01/09/2019
 It is unfortunate that we keep coming back to this same explanation concerning PCGS handling of my missing coin. They say that the images, videos or photos can not be released to me. I request that 1) Allow a representative from the Better Business Bureau be allowed to review videos,photos and images, 2) Myself to just review the

videos, photos and images in their monitored presence, 3) A elected public official review the videos,photos and image evidence . And again this process will close the dispute. Sincerest , Mr, Leslie C. *****

Complaint Type: Problems with Product/Service Status:

Answered 10/08/2018

I submited 2 PCGS gold coin through an authorized dealer for their "guarantee service", what happen is one of the gold coin has big size corrosion and another has numerous edge/graffiti. Upon PCGS guarantee, PCGS should compensate me the fair market price for those 2 overgraded coin. The PCGS Shanghai office (a direct branch from PCGS headquarter) actually break one of the PCGS slab and did 'restoration' process on the coin without my acknowledgement and confirmation. **When I asked authorized dealer about it, they told me PCGS told them they contacted me directly to get my authorization which is a lie.** Try to reach PCGS customer service, they just ignore the email without providing any proof that what they did is authorized and told me they want to collect all the fee associated with the guarantee service. **My complain is about PCGS's action to change customer's submission against customer will and not follow up on the consequence and lied about the case.**

M Response 10/19/2018 See attached.

Customer Response 10/21/2018

 PCGS claims that they tried to contact me for this issue, which is a total lie. During the whole process after Sep 28th, like 10 days, there is no PCGS email and telephone call. I left David Talk message and call him at least 3 times through the PCGS customer service without any response. The only response I got is after I filed complains at both Chinese authority and BBB. What PCGS shown in this case is completely arrogant, lack of professionalism and scam like 'grading operation'. Here is the email response I gave to David Talk after BBB involes, hi, Dave It is good to hear from you back unfortunately I have to contact both China and US authority to push for some improvement. I was travelling so cannot go to meet Tanya at Shanghai office last Friday with the Chinese Market Supervision Administration officer so I agree with the settlement with one condition. 1. Since Tanya insist the grade of the original coins has no problem and stick to your standard and the whole thing is a 'mis-communication', I need a PCGS official statement claim those 2 coins are actually up to the PCGS and ANA standard with the original picture attached. 2. If PCGS finally feels the original grading actually has problem and admit the error here, please issue an statement also with the original picture claim it is a mistake, **I still don't understand why the hell your guys want to take advantage of the Chinese collector like this,** any shame from your 'director of international coin'??? if he still think this is a PCGS MS63 coin? If it is just between MS61 and MS63, I won't even bother to contact PCGS since it would be very difficult, but that is a MS63?? **Even Chinese officer with no coin knowledge just read your standard and search some PCGS sample picture can not agree.** BTW, the whole thing is on a live thread in coinsky forum with all the picture and communication data, and I feel your guys just miss a good opportunity to show Chinese collector how responsible the PCGS is.

Maocheng M Response 10/29/2018
PCGS Shanghai Operations Manager, Alfred ****, has been in communication with the customer and with the Chinese Market Supervision Administration Officer regarding this issue. We have agreed to refund the fees to the customer. Mr. **** is awaiting a response from the customer regarding the refund. This matter is being resolved in China between PCGS Shanghai and the customer.

Customer Response 10/30/2018
I sent PCGS email at 10/21/2018 and there is still no answer from them, what I asked is not only to refund the fee, also I should get an official statement about what happens, with the original coin picture and PCGS stands for their

grade. Till now I did not get any response

Complaint Type: Problems with Product/Service Status:
Resolved 04/27/2018
On March 29, 2018 I paid $69 to join the Professional Coin Grading Services (PCGS) Silver ********** Club, under Order No. ********* aka: ********** ********, Inc. By doing this allowed me privileges to send in coins for grading. Therefore I had four coins I sent in on March 29 2018 to have graded. These four coins were in another coin grading company's holders therefore, PCGS would have to break them out in order to grade them and insert them into their holders. Per a discussion with ***** (customer service) at ###-###-####, Ext *** this was to happen. However when I received my coins back only two of the coins were taken out of the original holders and inserted into PCGS holders. The other two coins were not and no explanation as to why they were returned was ever sent to me. On April 24, 2018 I contacted a representative at PCGS (name unknown male) and advised him that I received an email 4/23 stating: Your order ******* shipped via USPS. Delivery Confirmation Number: 9**********77**********8. Thereafter I sent an email back to PCGS on 4/24/2018 stating: 1 1 ******** **** ****-D $1 Buffalo DNC USA 2 1 ******** 9**** ****-P $1 Buffalo, DC DNC USA 3 1 35389870 6800 1964 50C PR66 USA 4 1 35389871 5189 1996-W 10C MS66 USA However, he really couldn't share any light on what the DNC really means on the two buffalo coins. I did explain that the low grades on the two IGS (international Grading Service) coins were sort of surprising to me as they were graded 70's. But from what I have heard this company is selling a whole bunch of coins graded 70's and apparently getting away with swindling the general publics. Your graders have proven this by downgrading the two coins from 70's to 66. It would be nice if someone could like PCGS or NGC would sue or make these coins grading companies held accountable for their actions. I also told the customer service person I have seen this IGS coins selling on several coin shows with high grades, which most likely are rip offs. This coin grading companies and others are just hurting good companies like PCGS/NGC; (however, I respect ANACS I think they are reputable), but the others I don't think so. Heck maybe the are all-bad who knows, maybe have a big contest to find out the best, but we know that won't fly. As stated to the customer service representative only a high tech coin grading machine would make the playing field level. Back to my original question, that the customer service representative couldn't give me a definite answer on and that is what is DNC grade mean on the buffalo's? He stated there were no notes and could only speculate, but I want a clear definition on why the graders didn't have a grade on these coins. I know when I sent these coins into you folks they looked very clean and I didn't see anything wrong with them and I suspect ICG (Independent Coin Graders) didn't see a real noticeable imperfection with them either otherwise they would of graded them less than 70's. Anyway please provide me with the reason(s) these buffalo commemorative coins didn't grade out period, so that I can pass the information onto the next buyer I sell them to. **PCGS never replied to my 4/24/2018 email therefore, I sent two more emails to customer service and info@pcgs.com for status report on my inquiry. As of this complaint filing no one has responded to my original email dated 4/24/2018.** I did email them back again to advise them I would be contacting the BBB for action. Also after PCGS graded the two IGS coins the 50 cent Kennedy half dollar and 10 cent Roosevelt dime the value on both coins really took a hit and went down due to the PCGS grades of PF66 on the Kennedy and MS66 on the Roosevelt dime. Based upon PCGS price guide the value of the Kennedy in PF70 is $2,850 and the Roosevelt in MS70 is unknown, as no graded MS70 dime exists in any other grading company except for IGS. There is no way to tell the price, as IGS doesn't have a price guide. PCGS price guide for a MS69 is $350 so one would have to assume it would be way above that price. Since PCGS downgraded my coins they are only worth in the 66 grades for the Kennedy $21 and the Roosevelt $28 (PCGS price guide). As you can see the disparity really dropped the value of the IGS coins.

D Response 05/03/2018
PCGS is a division of ********** ******** which is a publicly traded company. In the 32 years since PCGS's founding, ********** ******** has graded and authenticated over 67 million items *wow!! another BS defence story as usual,* for a combined current value of over $32 billion. The nature of our business is that customers submit their coins and other collectibles to us for authentication and grading services. In this instance, the

customer submitted coins to PCGS that were previously graded by another Third-Party Grading Service and requested that they be put into PCGS holders. When a coin is submitted to PCGS that is already graded by another Grading Service, this is considered a "Crossover." Crossovers are reviewed by multiple PCGS Grading Experts including a Senior Grade/Verifier. If PCGS's Grading Experts do not believe the coin in question would qualify for the same grade in a PCGS holder, the coin would not be removed from its holder and would be returned to the customer as is. We've contacted the customer directly via email, our response to the customer is below; Good Afternoon Mr. ******, My name is ***** ****, I am the Customer Service Manager for PCGS. Your email was forwarded to me as soon as my team saw it in our email inbox. I apologize if this response is later than you expected, we receive a very high volume of calls and emails every day and we do our best to respond to each as quickly as possible. I reviewed your email below, your BBB complaint regarding this order, the notes my team left on the order and I have spoken with the Customer Service Representatives that you spoke with regarding this order. I apologize if my team was not able to provide a full and adequate response as to why your coins did not cross. As to "DNC" – this stands for "Did Not Cross' and is typically indicated on a Crossover that our graders did not feel met or exceeded whatever the minimum grade for that specific coin was based on PCGS's standards. I believe there was a bit of confusion or miscommunication on what exactly you wanted as a minimum grade for each coin. Based on your submission form, you requested "ANY" which is any numerical grade from 1 to 70, however on the letter you provided with the order you stated, "if by chance you folks grade either one of them lesser than a 70, please do not crack out, but send them back in the ICG holders." I know that you spoke with a few of our Customer Service Representatives and the Receiving Associate who processed your order after the submission was received, however the issue seems to have not been fully corrected prior to the order being completed and shipped back to you. I am going to have one of our Customer Service Representatives send you an email with instructions on how to return the coins to PCGS that did not cross, they will also provide you a pre-paid and fully insured FedEx mailing label to return the coins to us for us to continue to review them. If for some reason you're not able to print the label, please let me know or let the Customer Service Representative that emails the label to you know and we will print and mail a physical label to you. Please reply to this email stating you are ok crossing the coins into PCGS holders at ANY numerical grade prior to sending them back, this way I can be sure we're processing the order how you would like. As to PCGS's Grading Standards in general, PCGS is known as the "Standard for the Rare Coin Industry" and also as the most conservative grading service in the industry. This is typically why PCGS holders fetch a much higher premium than coins graded by other Third Party Grading Services out on the market. With PCGS being considered more conservative than other Third Party Grading services, our opinion will vary from the other services and we will not always agree with their opinion. Although ICG or IGS may have graded your specific coins as a 70, PCGS did not agree with that grade based on our standards. For future orders of crossover submissions, you have a few options as to when PCGS will remove your coins from their crossover holder and put them into a PCGS holder; ● Crossing at the same grade ○ If you do not list a minimum grade in the "Minimum Grade" column on the submission form, the numerical grade listed on the graded holder will be considered your minimum grade ○ If PCGS's Grading Experts do not believe the coin will cross at the current or a higher grade based on PCGS's standards, the coin will not be removed from its holder and will not be placed into a PCGS holder ● Crossing at a lower minimum grade ○ If you choose to do so, you can specify a minimum grade lower than the grade currently on the holder. For example, if your coin is currently in an MS65 holder but you would accept an MS62, you would list MS62 in the minimum grade column for that specific coin. You cannot specify a minimum grade higher than the current grade listed on the holder. ○ If PCGS's Grading Experts believe your coins is an MS62 or higher, we will remove the coin from its holder and will place it into a PCGS holder. If you list a specific minimum grade and PCGS believes the coin's grade should be higher than that, PCGS will place the coin into a PCGS holder with the grade our Grading Experts believe the coin qualifies for based on PCGS's standards ○ If the coin is deemed as "Genuine, Not Gradable" (explained in the next bullet point), PCGS would not remove that coin from its holder and it would not be placed into a PCGS holder. ● If crossing at "ANY" grade ○ If you write "ANY" in the minimum grade column for a crossover, PCGS will remove the coin from the other Grading Service's holder and will place it into a PCGS holder as long as our Grading Experts feel the coin warrants a numerical grade anywhere from 01 to 70. If a coin is deemed "Genuine, Not

Gradeable," the coin will not be removed from the crossover holder and will not be placed into a PCGS Holder. ○ "Genuine, Not Gradeable" coins are coins that are authentic but because of a problem, PCGS is not able to numerically grade them. For example, a coin may be authentic and numerically graded by another Grading Service but if PCGS believes the coin has been cleaned, damaged, or falls into one of our other "No Grade" codes, even if you state "ANY" as the minimum grade the coin will not be removed from its holder and placed into a PCGS holder. ● If crossing as "GENUINE" ○ If you indicate "GENUINE" in the minimum grade column on the submission form, PCGS will remove your coin from its holder and place it into a PCGS holder as long as it is authentic and does not have any of the following issues: ❑ Coin is counterfeit ❑ Coin has PVC (Polyvinylchloride) on the coin ❑ The lamination of the coin is peeling ❑ Our Grading Experts are not able to render a 100% opinion on a coin For additional information on our "No Grade" codes/reasons and PCGS's Grading Standards in general, please visit www.PCGS.com/Grades. I hope that I have been able to address each of your concerns and/or questions with this email. I will be responding to your BBB complaint with an opening statement followed by the full text of this email. If my offer to have you return the coins, that did not cross, to PCGS to cross them and my other responses in this email are to your satisfaction, please respond to the BBB complaint once you receive the updated email from them and confirm that you are satisfied with PCGS's response. If you have any questions or need additional information, please let me know.

Customer Response 05/04/2018 Better Business Bureau:
I have reviewed the response made by the business in reference to complaint ID ********, and have determined that this proposed action would not resolve my complaint. For your reference, details of the offer I reviewed appear below. [Provide details of why you are not satisfied with this resolution. Please respond in this space ONLY] Regards, *** ****** I received an email from ***** ****, Customer Service Manager stating he would be responding back to you folks with the same email he sent to me. Although I do not 100% agree with Mr. **** email my concerns are: 1. I will not be sending back the two ICG **** P Buffalo Commemorative PF70, DCAM and the ICG **** D Buffalo Combative MS70 coins because after my experience with the two perfect IGS coins the 50 cent Kennedy half dollar and 10 cent Roosevelt dime the value on both coins really took a hit and went down due to the PCGS grades of PF66 on the Kennedy and MS66 on the Roosevelt dime. Based upon PCGS price guide the value of the Kennedy in PF70 is $2,850 and the Roosevelt in MS70 is unknown, as no graded MS70 dime exists in any other grading company except for IGS. There is no way to tell the price, as IGS doesn't have a price guide. PCGS price guide for a MS69 is $350 so one would have to assume it would be way above that price. Since PCGS downgraded my coins they are only worth in the 66 grades for the Kennedy $21 and the Roosevelt $28 (PCGS price guide). As you can see the disparity really dropped the value of the IGS coins. Therefore, it was a good thing there was an alleged miscommunication/confusion issue between ***** Salgado on the submission information; otherwise PCGS would have cracked open the Buffalo coins holders as Mr. **** email suggest. PCGS would have devalued and lowered the grade of the Buffalo coins as they done to the ICG coins. Although I believe there was no miscommunication and Mr. Salgado understood what I wanted. If the conversation was recorded than Mr. **** can review the conversation. But in the end it was good thing that PCGS took the low road and sent back the two ICG coins unmolested with the perfect grades intact. 2. Although not mentioned I would like for PCGS to send me the notes or whatever information they have in grading the two IGS coins. I would like to review their notes regarding the reason(s) both coins were down graded 4 points on the Sheldon coin grading scale. If I were to send both coins back to IGS with these notes and IGS took them out of the PCGS holders and graded them less than perfect 70's again, one could speculate a switch may have happened. However, if IGS were to grade them the same as before perfect 70's than that negates a switch took place. It's back to them versus us in the grading game. Or we are bigger and better than you. As Mr. **** stated: "Although ICG or IGS may have graded your specific coins as a 70, PCGS did not agree with that grade based on our standards." That is what I am ****ing about its the them versus us scenario. Its only human nature and Mr. **** would agree if you were to put one coin grader from all grading companies into a room and pass around the same coin that there would not be a 100% consensus (in a secret vote) on the coin grade. Some would grade the coin differently than another grader and visa versa. As indicated by a reputable numismatics: I believe someone will eventually invent an affordable

computer option to all collectible grading as long as the majority focuses on the financial end of hobby collecting versus the true ********** end. They have already done it with the music industry with auto tune. Maybe in the end computerization is the answer, which would eliminate the human factor. That would make sense and create a level playing field. No coin grade could ever be disputed again. It makes sense but could it happen, NO as it would turn into a city hall fight scenario. 3. Lastly, Mr. **** did explain my question on the "Did Not Cross" item. In closing I request to cancel my subscription and would like a refund. If the refund were returned than I would consider this case closed, even though I am accepting as it stands. Also, I have no choice but to absorb the loss in value on the two downgraded coins. Chalk this up as a learning experience and Caveat emptor in the coin grading business.

D Response 05/07/2018
Based on the large volume of coins graded each day at PCGS, our graders are not able to leave notes on each individual coin. They indicate their opinion of each coin when inputting the grade, no grade and or designation(s) into our internal PCGS grading system. We would not be able to provide Mr. ****** with any other information or notes other than that the two coins returned in their original holders did not cross. As to Mr. ******'s statement of a possible coin switch, PCGS keeps no inventory on-hand other than what customers send us to grade. After over 32 years of operating, (stealing), PCGS has multiple and extensive procedures in place to ensure a coin is not mishandled at any time during our process. The coins submitted to PCGS are the coins that were returned to Mr. ******. PCGS Memberships are non-refundable however based on Mr. ******'s request, we have started the refund process to have the full $69 refunded back to his original form of payment. Typically, if cancelling a membership, the customer's submission privileges are removed as well as they no longer have a valid membership, for Mr. ****** we will keep his access active until the end of his original membership term, 3/29/2018. Once the original membership term expires, Mr. ****** will have the option of renewing his membership manually or allowing it to lapse.

Customer Response 05/07/2018
[A default letter is provided here which indicates your acceptance of the business's response. If you wish, you may update it before sending it.] Better Business Bureau: I have reviewed the response made by the business in reference to complaint ID ********, and find that this resolution would be satisfactory to me. I will wait for the business to perform this action and, if it does, will consider this complaint resolved. Regards, *** ****** Mr. ****: I will accept PCGS offer but (if possible) would **like to see more transparency from the company regarding notes etc., on coins graded. Without the notes etc, etc., one has no proof as to why the grader(s) lowered my coins from high value, perfect 70's to low value 66s. No proof whatsoever, it leaves a customer scratching his head as to how they came to their decision. With notes etc., its called transparency and without that it smells like a red herring.**

Complaint Type: Problems with Product/Service
Status: Resolved 01/17/2018
This company, PCGS, certifies coins. PCGS inspects a coin, certifies its authenticity, and then places the coin into a plastic container. The container is sealed shut and it can only be opened by breaking the container. This certification increases the value of the coin. Really??

In December 2017, someone gave me a coin as a gift. The coin was certified, in a sealed container, by PCGS and the approximate value of the coin is $325. I don't know whether my friend purchased the coin directly from PCGS. Upon my receipt of the coin, I noticed that the container had two imperfections in it. (An imperfection lessens the value of the coin.) **I contacted PCGS and was told to send the coin to PCGS so they could replace the damaged container. (If the customer replaces the cover, the certification will be void.) I mailed the coin to PCGS on 12/13/17 and I received the coin back on 1/11/18. When I got the coin back, I noticed that the container was still damaged (i.e., PCGS only fixed one of the two imperfections.) I immediately brought this**

to the attention of PCGS and told them that I would like this to be fixed but that I don't want to have to wait another month---since I already waited a month. I was told that the manager would have to call me back. I left numerous messages for the manager and he has not called me back; it has been approximately 6 days since I brought this to the attention of PCGS.

M Response 03/15/2018
PCGS is a division of Collectors Universe which is a publicly traded company. In the 32 years since PCGS's founding, Collectors Universe has graded and authenticated over 68 million items for a combined current value of over $35 billion. same old broken record, The nature of our business is that customers submit their coins and other collectibles to us for authentication and grading services. In this instance, this customer received a PCGS-graded coin as a gift. In the customer's complaint, he mentioned that he was unsure if his friend purchased the coin directly from PCGS or not. PCGS does not buy or sell coins, we strictly authenticate and grade them. The coin was most likely purchased from another coin collector or from a PCGS Authorized Dealer online or in Mr. ********* Friend's local area. Mr. ******* noticed two small blemishes or imperfections on the inner gasket of the PCGS holder (an inner plastic gasket holds the coin inside of and in place in the PCGS holder). Mr. ******* contacted PCGS regarding the issue he observed on the holder. PCGS requested images as is our normal procedure to ensure that customers are not sending PCGS-holdered coins back to PCGS for "correction" if they are correct and in the appropriate condition. We informed Mr. ******* that small blemishes such as the ones he had mentioned were not uncommon but we would still work with him to attempt to correct the issue once images were received as he was not satisfied with the current condition of the holder and gasket. Once images of the coin holder issue were received, we provided Mr. ******* with a pre-paid and fully insured FedEx label along with step-by-step instructions on how to send the coin to PCGS so that we could review the issue in-person and potentially correct it. Upon receiving the coin at PCGS, the coin was reviewed by one of PCGS's most senior experts. The coin in question was correct as-is with no issue other than two small blemishes on the inner gasket. The coin was removed from the PCGS holder and gasket and placed into a new PCGS gasket then into a new PCGS holder. The PCGS holder was then sonically sealed by PCGS personnel. Prior to the coin being shipped back to Mr. *******, the PCGS Customer Service Representative that was working with Mr. ******* personally reviewed the coin and holder in question along with our Operations Personnel. They determined the blemish that Mr. ******* had referred to on the PCGS holder/gasket was no longer on this new gasket. The coin was then sent back to Mr. *******, once again on PCGS's account, fully insured and at no cost to Mr. *******. Once Mr. ******* received the coin back he was still not satisfied with the PCGS holder. At this point, Mr. ******* contacted PCGS Customer Service again and proceeded to inform our staff that he was not satisfied with the correction and felt that the issue had not been resolved. Mr. ******* was advised that if he was still not satisfied with the small imperfection on the inner plastic he could send it back to PCGS again on our account and at no charge to him for us to review the holder again but Mr. ******* did not want to go this route. All plastic used for PCGS holders, gaskets and any material that PCGS uses are of very specific materials and compositions to ensure that they cannot harm any coin or collectible that is placed into a PCGS holder. Once a coin is placed into a PCGS holder it is typically not removed, extreme amounts of research and care go into developing all materials used by PCGS to ensure the safe storage of the coin or other collectible over time. Throughout the process used to manufacture PCGS materials, very small blemishes or imperfections can sometimes be found in the outer areas of PCGS holders and/or gaskets. These small imperfections by no means affect the value of the PCGS-graded coin as they are on the PCGS holder and not the coin itself. As previously stated, PCGS does not buy or sell coins, thus we would not be able to exchange the coin in question. During the very beginning process of assisting Mr. *******, we did let him know that typically if there is an issue such as this, the coin can be exchanged through the person that the coin was purchased from. Sometimes for the consumer this is easier and quicker than sending the coin back to PCGS directly. If Mr. ******* would like to send the coin back to PCGS, I personally, along with our Operations Manager, will hand select the plastic holder and inner gasket to replace the current holder and gasket when placing the coin into a new PCGS holder. We cannot guarantee that there may or may not still be a very small blemish on the plastic as is common.

M Response 03/20/2018

PCGS will contact the customer via email to provide a FedEx return label. We will review and attempt to correct the issue as quickly as possible. I will place an alert on the customer's PCGS account internally so that when the order is received at PCGS I will be notified so that I can walk the order through the process.

Customer Response 03/22/2018 Better Business Bureau:
 I have reviewed the response made by the business in reference to complaint ID ********, and find that this resolution would be satisfactory to me. I will wait for the business to perform this action and, if it does, will consider this complaint resolved. PCGS SHOULD RECEIVE THE COIN WITHIN 24 HOURS. IF I RECEIVE THE COIN BACK BY 4/6/2018, EVERYTHING WILL BE SATISFACTORY. Regards, ***** *******

complaint below from Felix Diaz Artista, He sent me 137 pages PDF of his case !!!
Félix Díaz Artista

This is so sad to happen and should be investigated !!! He lives in mexico, Why doesnt the ANA do something about all these claims ??? are they paid off too ? Or do they fear PCGS ?? OR THE AUCTION HOUSES ??

<u>Collectors Universe</u> - PCGS damaged my coins after I refused to sell 3 of them.

AdvertisementsSome advertisers may pay us for this ad to appear on our website or provide us with a referral fee. Our content is free because we may earn a commission if you purchase products after clicking ads on our website.

Oct 18, 2019

Verified Reviewer

This review is from a real person who provided valid contact information and hasn't been caught misusing, spamming or abusing our website. Check our FAQ

1 comment

1.0

Details

PCGS & Collectors Universe as well, damaged 5 coins of mine. The absurd comes as that coins were previously graded an imaged by them, then I sent them for restoration.

After 4 months and no news and answers to my emails, they said coins have down graded, and offer me to purchase. I said no, because I knew my coins were so good and they were just trying to cheat on me. They got mad and sent back my coins fully damaged. They imaged the damaged coins.

So I have true view images before and after, were damages are clear as water. Those are their own images, no way they can allege images do not correspond to the coins.

This case can destroy the PCGS for good, but I live in Mexico and nobody seems to care. I have all evdences, email with deceits from Rosenberg, the mudy process, everything.

Reason of review: Damaged or defective.
Monetary Loss: $100,000
Preferred solution: I want the potencial price the coins could reach if not damaged. They did a crime. They intented a fraud..
Collectors Universe Cons: Are capable of the worst.

Check out this next coin toned purple, wow, does anybody have a logical explanation about this tone ?? and why it was even graded ??

I read that a popular method of cooking a coin is with a blowtorch and using borax to alter its color, this coin looks definatley artificialy toned.

<u>**AFFIDAVIT & QUESTIONAIRE**</u>

On a phone call received march 26 4:45 PM EST which was recorded, mr
Rosenberg told me "I'll make it right with you" , if the coin was not the original one sent in,

On an email received from David Rosenberg he communicated the message below

 Here is my contact info… Any pictures you have before/after are appreciated.

Thank you,

David Rosenberg
VP, Operations
Collectors Universe, Inc.
949-567-1203
Tue, Mar 26, 2019 6:29 pm EST

On march 27ᵗʰ 1:04 pm EST I sent 7 pictures by email showing the difference in the coin they
sent me vs my original one that I had sent in,

To:DRosenberg Details Slideshow
**As the pictures show the coin sent back to me is clearly not my coin, the first pics are
my coin, and then the pics of the one in the PCGS holder has multiple contact marks
among a very noticable scratch in front of jefferson's nose also mine had full steps and
the one in the PCGS holder does not, the lustre is different also, in the next email ill
show you another fraud where PCGS graded a nickel and gave it a "FS" designation
when there are nicks and scratches and separation marks ALL OVER THE
STEPS !!!!!!!! and it has a CAC label also ??????? this is crazy !!!!!!!!! there are other
coins of fraud i have found, and its sickening, as you have stated to me mr rosenberg
"PCGS has graded over 40 million coins" well that doesnt mean a dam thing when
fraud exists EVERYWHERE and now even the well experienced collectors on youtube
are exposing the fraud of PCGS, this current information is not speculation but fact,
and ive only been researching for less than a week, !!!
seeing how PCGS sent me back a MS65 nickel loaded with scratches and no FS, by all
means my original one i sent in should have graded MS67+ UPWARDS !!!! and
somebody must have noticed that super fine example , they must have really thought
they could get away with taking it for thierself thinking who knows what ???**

On the same day march 27ᵗʰ @ 3:16 pm EST mr Rosenberg replied by email as my

On the next pages I provided more examples of real complaints I found in 2019 and included them in my complaint to the court. Included are email communication from myself and david rosenberg I am not a law student and have no training with legal matters but I did the best I could just in case a lawyer wanted to take my case. I had even the summons filled out for the 3 criminals in CA. There's no way I could proceed with this alone.

records show below, at this point mr Rosenberg <u>lied</u> to me, He said he would make it right with me if I showed the picture evidence which I had done as he requested, Now he is trying to get back the coin without valid reason.

Mr. Suval -

Thank you for sending these images. The other emails you sent are unrelated to the issue at hand.

What I'd like to do i have you return to PCGS the nickel in question so that we can see it up close and compare it to the images that we have of the coin.

This will be done at no cost to you, I've CC'd Joseph Pielago here and he can arrange to get you a prepaid FedEx label so that you can send the coin back at our cost.

Also - with regard to your credit card declining, I cannot offer an explanation for why that happened, and I've asked the Accounting team to try again.

Furthermore for the two coins you have in house, I had our variety experts confirm their opinions of the coin.

Thank you

below is my reply, march 27th 4:32 pm EST [partial email]

I **will not** send back the 1956 nickel because it is evidence in a criminal investigation, now for numerous times; and im asking again to show the reason with CLARITY for the delay of my 2 coins sent in for a 5 day express service, there is NO evidence of ANY "declined" financial transaction as stated by yourself and tyler for being a reason of a delay on my 5 day express order. I have provided you with the full records for the month of march showing the card is active with funds available, I also double checked my submission form and the math looked correct to me, there was never any explanation of asking me for extra money anyways, even you did not provide an explanation of the "extra charge" that was alledgedy "declined" the whole story has no merit or fact. so if you would please enlighten me on the cause for the extra charge? that would be nice,
To this current time now **I would like for you to show me any professional service or expertise** that I have recieved by PCGS. please do so.

regards, troy

march 28th 9:29 am EST my writing to mr Rosenberg asking him what is wrong with the pictures and he will not answer,

"theres absolutely nothing wrong with the images!! explain to me what is wrong with the images ?? plenty of people have already seen the images and the coin, theres no problem with clarity and no mistake, you told me you "would make it right with me" if I sent in images>which I have done, now youre telling me another story that you want the coin [nickel] back ? and provided no reason with MERIT, the nickel sent back to me from PCGS IT IS CLEARLY NOT MY NICKEL !! "

"Sir - if you're not willing to send the coin back to us for us to review the images, then our conversation is over.

I have provided you with a way to potentially rectify the situation and you've chosen not to participate. *LIE !!! you have not provided no way,,, the only motive you show is to try to get back the evidence, I have sent the clear pictures as you r equested*
If you'd like to continue this conversation I can direct you to our attorney.

With regards to your other order, if it didn't ship today, it will ship tomorrow.

David"

march 28th 1:48 pm EST,
 mr Rosenberg **lied again**, he said he was going to ship my coins graded, but now he is going to send them back not graded and cancel my yearly subscription? Seems he went into a temper tantrum because I would not send back the coin,

on march 28th 1:47 pm EST mr Rosenberg writes;
 "The coins in order 21569231 have been removed from the PCGS holders and will be returned to you raw at no cost to you. Furthermore, any remaining balance you have on your PCGS Collectors Club membership will be refunded. You should see these refunds over the next week"

Mr Rosenberg NEVER GAVE A REASON WHAT WAS WRONG WITH THE PICTURES WHEN I HAD MANY PEOPLE SEE THE PICTURES EVEN A PRINT/COPY SPECIALIST WORKS AT STAPLES FOR OVER TEN YEARS !!!!! Mr Rosenberg said he "would make it right with me" then makes numerous attempts to get back the evidence and then has a hissy-fit because he has been out-smarted, so now he acts out in spitefullness and revenge with his fancy words thinks it portrays innocence,
===

march 28th 1:47 pm EST,
 this whole fabrication below is not true, from the evidence and numerous complaints ive seen about PCGS this cannot be true, the images already have been compared of my original coin I purchased from ebay with the one sent back to me, any problems with not being able to determine the major differences [not the same coin] would have me to believe somebody is mentally retarded, or blind, or a fraudster trying to get back the evidence, the whole statement below is without merit and is smoke and mirrors by common sense and basic logic

"The reason I asked for photos was because in quite literally 100% of the instances where Ive been involved with a customer suggesting that a coin had been swapped, we have been able to prove without doubt that the coins were in fact not swapped – simply by comparing the customer's original image with the coin in the PCGS holder.

I asked to have the coin physically returned so that we could remove the coin from the holder and photograph it raw,[*ARE YOU BLIND??!!!*] so that we could better compare the "before" and "after" images. You've refused to work with me".*LIE>>I sent you the images you asked for, and you also refused to discuss the value of my nickel and told me it was not important. Mr Rosenberg claims literally 100% that he proves customer coins were not swapped, when on the contrary the extensive amount of complaints online and my pictures prove otherwise, and in some cases the same scenerio as my case with him going silent refusing to speak and directing people to their attorney,*

"*Fraud:* An intentional perversion of truth

I see by the case below and others how david rosenberg handles complaints,

PCGS coin grading service //Collectors Universe // David Rosenberg Stole a rare coin, replaced with other, relabeled holder fake label not the 47k coin i sent value of coin returned $61.00 Newport Beach, CA Internet // Cal.// Illinois

I had joined PCGS coingrading service to have my high end and some rare coins graded handed down by my father.

I had researched for weeks before paying a $149.00 membership fee as worried on losing my $47,000 coin for grading as i read BBB had some simalar reports.

Idid it as i thought ok, its safe nothing bad will happen.

I sent my rare coin after taking pictures and comparisons to other coins that look the same but not rare as this one particcular coin.

I paid a grading fee of $192.00 and my shipping of $32.00 with insurance.

I finally received my coin much later than paid for and it had the label and what i expected a 1964 SP GRADE 68

I was using it as collateral for a small loan but the lender said the numbers on the coin label did not match PCGS web site for that coin.

I called them and after researching this my self with no response from the company i eventually found the label on the front of coin holder was crooked so a peeled it back a little to see another label underneath, inside the holder stating a different coin as worth $61. [continued below]....

....00

SOMEONE HAD SWAPPED MY COIN AND SENT A DIFFERENT COIN BUT DID NOT CHANGE THE LABEL ONLY TO ADD A LABEL OVER THE TOP OF THE HOLDER.

I had tried to work with the company V.P. David Rosenberg but he referred me to their atty and then tried sending me a $21.00 check after requesting cancellation of membership ($149.00) and my coin. nothing was done by him, the atty or anyone. Atty Kieth Attelsey never responded to me or my calls.

I have filed complaint with BBB, State of Cal. Atty general and State atty general in South Dakota where i live.

I am now going to pursue major legal action as i have the proof of my real coin, their coin not the same and a video and pictures of the fake label placed over the holder.

I want my refunds of over $350.00 and i want my coin or at least a replacment of equal value!!

I would never send coins to this company read the BBB reports and research them before wanting to do busness.

David C. Hicks

This report was posted on Ripoff Report on 03/09/2017 12:04 PM and is a permanent record located here: https://www.ripoffreport.com/reports/pcgs-coin-grading-service/internet/pcgs-coin-grading-service-collectors-universe-david-rosenberg-stole-a-rare-coin-re-1360764. The posting time indicated is Arizona local time. Arizona does not observe daylight savings so the post time may be Mountain or Pacific depending on the time of year. Ripoff Report has an exclusive license to this report. It may not be copied without the written permission of Ripoff Report. READ: Foreign websites steal our content

QUESTIONS:

What was/is wrong with the pictures I provided of my original coin and the coin sent to me from PCGS? EXPLAIN WITH CLARITY !!!

Why did mr Rosenberg want to remove the coin from its holder to see it better as he stated to me? Does he have vision problems? I already told him how many people seen the pictures and the coin., I have a german [karl zeiss] lens on my camera by the way.

Why did mr Rosenberg make numerous attempts to get back the coin after he agreed to "make it right with me"? Thats called LYING !!!! AND THE FABRICATION> ALLEDGING THERES SOMETHING WRONG WITH THE PICTURES WHEN THERES NOTHING WRONG WITH THOSE PICTURES !!!!!

Why was my yearly membership canceled? What articulable reason for canceling my yearly membership?

Why did I pay for a 5 day express service [for my two 1943 coins] and my coins were "in house" for over 3 weeks?? what is the explanation?

Why am I seeing numerous similar complaints on different websites of coin swapping [stealing] by PCGS?, and mr Rosenberg canceling peoples subscriptions? AND FOR WHAT REASON ???

Have I ever received any professional service or expertise from PCGS ? If so, please explain to me with relevance,

Since when is it a policy of PCGS to cancel a yearly subscription because of someone that has a complaint or grievance?

Since when is it wrong to threaten a lawsuit when somebody steals my property?

Have I done anything wrong? If so, you may write it in affidavit form and send it to me, please use common english and not legalese.

Respondent to Respondent, must respond within 14 days. Please provide relevance and clarity with your response.

Silence can only be equated with fraud where there is a legal or moral duty to speak or where an inquiry left unanswered would be intentionally misleading. [US v. Tweel, 550 F.2d 297, 299 (1977) quoting US v. Prudden, 424 F 2d 1021, 1032 (1970)]

Silence is a species of conduct, and constitutes an implied representation of the existence of the state of facts in question, and the estoppel is accordingly a species of estoppel by misrepresentation. [cite omitted] when silence is of such a character and under such circumstances that it would become a fraud upon the other party to permit the party who has kept silent to deny that which his silence has induced the other to believe and act upon, it will operate as estoppel. [Carmine v. Bowen, 64 A. 932 (1906)]

Your silence stands a consent, and tacit approval, for the declarations of facts and conclusions here being established as fact, as a law matter and this affidavit absent timely rebutal, will stand as final judgment in this matter.

Failure to reply within 14 days, establishes you are in agreement with the foregoing and are thusly legally estopped pursuant to: Carmine v. Bowen, 64 A. 932, 1906, silence activates estoppel.

I, troy sumal, hereby reserve the right to amend this letter /document, and am the only party authorized to assert the right to make amendments to this document as necessary, and in order that the truth may be ascertained and these proceedings justly determined. Should any party possess information that will controvert and overcome this Declaration with specificity, please advise Me in writing by DECLARATION in AFFIDAVIT FORM within

14, days from receipt hereof and thereby, provide Me with your timely rebutal, proving with particularity by stating all requisite actual evidentiary fact and all requisite actual law, and at no time in reliance on mere presumptive facts and personal conclusions law, that this Affidavit by Verified Declaration is substantially and materially false sufficiently for changing materially my declaration.

The Undersigned, I, troy sumal, do herewith declare, state and say that I, troy sumal with sincere intent in truth, that I, the undersigned am competent by stating the matters set forth herein, that the contents are true, correct, complete, and certain, admissible as evidence, reasonable, not misleading, and by My best knowledge, by Me, the undersigned. This document and all others pertaining to this issue may be recorded and thusly may be used at the discretion of its issuer for any and all matters as so allowed under Rule 902 of the Federal Rules of Evidence and others, including, without limitations, the jurisdiction of the State of florida, florida state, and the United States of America.

By my hand, this 16th of April, 2019,

 troy sumal,   UCC 1-308   all rights reserved

troy sumal   954-770-8524, antiquefineartt@aol.com

ZIP EXEMPT

PLAINTIFF :

troy joseph sumal
 3200 NW 62 AVE STE 30
Margate, Florida state
33063
954 770 8524

DEFENDANT[S] :

COLLECTORS UNIVERSE

PCGS
Entity Address:
1610 E. ST. ANDREW PL
SANTA ANA CA 92705
Entity Mailing Address:
PO BOX 6280
NEWPORT BEACH CA 92658
+1 949.567.1234

CAUSE OF ACTION
[includes two separate complaints]

GENERAL ALLEGATIONS

(Against All Defendants)

REGISTERED AGENT> Michelle Taylor &

Collectors Universe, CEO Ron Orlando, PCGS coin grading service, V.P. Director David Rosenberg,

I.

STEALING

[felony theft]

II.

FRAUD

III.

MULTIPLE LYING

IV.

DISHONEST PRACTICES

V.

UNPROFESSIONAL CONDUCT

VI.

MALICE

VII.

DEFAMATION OF MY COINS

[3 washington quarters]

VIII.

BREECH OF CONTRACT

X.

FALSE AND MISLEADING STATEMENTS

XI

INTENTIONAL INFLICTION OF EMOTIONAL DISTRESS

XII

NEGLEGENCE

Once the General Allegations have been established, the 3-Step Cause of Action is used for each Claim being made. For instance, if negligence and negligence per se are the two claims, the writer would go through the 3-Step Cause of Action twice, once for each claim.

THE CLAIMS:

FACTS:
On March 2nd, 2019, I sent in 5 coins, consisting of the following: 1956-P nickel with full steps, 1964-D quarter, 1956 quarter, 1963-D quarter and 1964-D quarter To PCGS Coin grading service which is a sub-franchise of collectors universe, tracking # 9405518995560034107133. [Declared value 14,000 low estimate]

I paid 234.95 + 7.90 USPS mailing cost for the service of coin grading and return within 2 weeks return time of my 5 coins. The coins were returned on time.

Upon getting my coins back I noticed the Jefferson nickel **was not** my nickel that I had sent in, also there were 3 washington quarters falsely labeled such as "questionable color", "details", and "ungradable "

The Jefferson nickel was not my nickel !!! as I have pics of the nickel I bought from ebay for proof and clearly the one I received back is not the same one. [anyways,I have no junky scratched up nickels in my collection !!! and its absurd !!!] and this one they sent back had scratches [contact marks] on both sides, and no "FS". [full steps] My 1956-P Jefferson nickel also had the full steps and was quite valuable, there were no scratches or contact marks on the obverse or reverse with a very strong strike.

The nickel they sent back to me along with one quarter received a same grade of MS65. The quarter had no scratches or contact marks but the nickel did on both sides and they were graded the same, very unusual and inconsistant,

I contacted PCGS/Collectors Universe by telephone on march 26th phone record below

03/26/2019 4:49PM 800-447-8848 Voice M2O 24 min Outgoing $0.00]
 immediatley after looking at the nickel that was not mine, and spoke to David Rosenberg [V.P.
Director] who told me If the nickel was not the same one I had sent in he would "make it right with
me" I emailed 7 pictures and he did not keep his word, the games begin now with mr Rosenberg.

When you call in to Collectors Universe, the recording says any and all calls may be recorded, and the
customer service representative did tell me all calls are recorded, so mr Rosenberg should be recorded
what he said to me on march 26 that he "would make it right with me if it is not the same coin"

the pictures prove it

I was told numerous times on email, also from attorney kieth attlesley I was refunded, and getting
refund[s], [received late refund on may 1st, 473.00], and only received a refund for my PCGS
membership, 69$ I received [by march 29th approx] and not the rest for 2 seperate submissions equaling
approx $453.00 and **especially need to be compensated** for a nickel worth $10,000 minimum +++ &
numerous other frauds & damages

V.P. Director David Rosenberg told me on email that he seen a video more than once of the video of my
original coin, well he never offered me to see that video, and one complaint online [another coin
swapping issue], a girl demanded to see a video of her coin and even sent in a freedom of information
act request [FOIA] and the video was refused to her, so why does he even bother mentioning such
video?

On april 16th mr V.P. Director David Rosenberg stated to me on an email he received two blurry
pictures from me, when on the contrary I sent him 7 clear pictures on march 27th, and kept asking what
is wrong with the pictures I sent? and he now responds 3 weeks later ?

COMPLAINT #1

The general alligations apply to this complaint along with the second complaint in this cause of action,
this complaint is for submission #5807341, order #21572485. [Declared value 14,000 minimum]i'm
very upset over the missing nickel and the other frauds and numerous mistakes by this [PCGS] alledged
"professional" coin grading service. Both submissions were totally screwed up !!! after numerous
emails with mr Rosenberg I found myself correcting him with many rebuttals because he takes
everything I say and twists it severely making it into lies or his own untrue conclusion or meanings., I
sent comparative prices of a coin sold for 9200.00 and my nickel looked better than that one, he
ignored it, I even showed a coin fraudulently graded by PCGS and he ignored it, we went back and
forth with emails where I asked him specifically "what is wrong with my pictures"? And he answers
over 3 weeks later with a lie[s] saying I sent 2 blury pics when I sent 7 clear pics, and he said they were
blury when they are not, mr Rosenberg tried his best effort to get back the evidence , and then when he
could not get back the junky nickel they sent me, he seemed to go into a tantrum at that point and
canceled my yearly subscription, [claiming it was because I threatened lawsuit], well I threatened that
the first day I spoke with him, why didnt he cancel my subscription then?? [probably because he

wanted to get back the nickel they sent me, thats what I think,] and refused to communicate, mr Rosenberg uses many adjectives and fancy words thinking it portrays innocence, so does kieth attlesey the attorney for collectors universe who tries to order me not to post complaints and talked to me like a mafia thug on the phone,

words like "personal attacks" "abusive" "hostile" "harrass" and more words twisting up contexts an twisting anything factual, and this is why I use the word **"LIAR". I have rebuttal emails proving what they say and how I corrected both of them, mr Rosenberg and Mr Attlesey, now ill just spend more time gathering up all the communications and get it all printed out**

my research online I see many people complaining of coins being switched {stolen} by PCGS of all [most]>which were submitting their coins for the first time like me, seems to be a pattern, I will provide all email communication with who said what, also on the submission #5807341 there were 3 quarters not graded, they were labeled, "questionable color" "details" "cleaned" and labeled "ungradable" on the back, I could not believe it !!!!!! my beautifully toned washington quarters !!!!!!!!! all defiled, and one quarter with a grade of MS65 which I think was undergraded. [because it had no scratches or contact marks], By the way, **HOW DO THESE "PROFESSIONALS" GRADE MY QUARTER MS65 WITH NO SCRATCHES OR CONTACT MARKS ON EITHER SIDE, AND GIVE THE SAME GRADE TO THE JUNKY NICKEL WITH SCRATCHES AND CONTACT MARKS ON BOTH SIDES?** Theres another fraud,

I sent in some of my best coins in order to pay my traffic fine and get my truck on the road and get a 14 foot enclosed trailer, surely the sale of these coins would have provided the funds I needed, now two orders were screwed up and im left with one quarter, MS65 which I have no choice but to put it in a action and get whatever I can because I am hurt financially, I borrowed money to get these coins graded costed about 473.00 and now I have been told I am getting refunds, mr Rosenberg said on email I have been refunded once ,and I should have already received one, and the other is on the way, he wrote to me last 7-9 days from today April 29th, another email I just seen from **april 6th** shows accounting looks like a 200$ refund?? not sure [see below]

"Dear troy joseph sumal,

For your records, attached is the invoice for your recent PCGS order.

If the balance due is zero, the order has been paid in full and no further action is required"

Order No.	Submission No.	Order Amount	Payment Amount	Balance Due
21572485	5807341	$200.00	$200.00	$0.00

[received late refund on may 1st 473.00]

I have no idea what theyre doing or done, but it takes 4-5 days for any mail [envelope] to come from CA. I will find the email message, now everytime I get a notice from my PMB private mailbox that I have received mail, I have to go over there hoping there is a check or checks because I need that money to start over again, it takes me 2 ½-3 hours or more to ride the bus to margate to my mailbox, and at least ten times I have done this looking for checks that arent there, [received late refund may 1st 473.00] meanwhile keeping a log journal of all the time spent on this case doing research, going to staples for copies and printouts and other legal studies taking up my time **WHEN MY TIME IS LIMITED ENOUGH AS IT IS !!!!!!! I dont have my truck on the road and I have to take the bus everywhere,,, its very stressfull now having this unexpected and unwanted fiasco with these ^% $#@##@@#$&&%#$% >>people I have to constantly fight for my property and frauds to be compensated and fight for righteousness, and justice, I was so sick the first week I couldnt hardly do anything, I had no strength, I had it all planned out to sell these coins and get my life back and get all my antiques and artworks and collectables to auctions & market[s], and get a better living conditions, ive been waiting a long time, but yet some crook has to pull their trix with my property and mess everything up causeing me severe havoc, I dont have time for anything in life, not even to watch a 5 minute coin video for study, no time to study coins, no time to look at my stamp collection, to contact auctions or buyers, no time to ride my bike, no time to list things for sale on offer up or craigslist, no time to study sub-penny stocks, etc etc etc etc etc,,,,,, its all my energy and time on this case now, I dont have internet where I live , so library is all I have and anywhere wheres there's a wifi during my daytime travels,, my life is at a stand still now,**

I attempted to communicate with David Talk of customer service still seeking remedy and compensation, or even investigation of my missing nickel, and I was directed back to mr Rosenberg where I hear from him and his attorney that I am being abusive, harrassing and hostile? I am only trying to get my property back or be compensated for it and discuss with somebody about all these frauds, but yet I am called all these words that are lies and making me to look like something I am not

I called PCGS asking about my refunds on the my phone record below. I was told by the accounting representative my refunds were initiated on april 5th and it would take 7-10 business days for me to receive them, here it is april 30th and not received, [received late refund may 1" 473,00] I have to send in more coins to another grader and start all over.
04/08/2019 11:59AM 800-447-8848 Voice M2O 3 min Outgoing $0.00

And I am told this is harrassing and abusive and hostile, when I was never hostile or any of the other fiction [lies] they are talking about, I told mr Attlesey to get the man or woman to come forth with such a claim, he is so full of it, both of them !!

If I have to sell any of my valuables in my antique collection or a silver dollar[s] for more paperwork and printout costs, or any other expense from this case, im making note of it for reimbursement, because my buget is so stretched right now im barely surviving, I dont have any family, and I borrowed money from a lady friend to get these coins graded, and im not borrowing any more.

What hurts me the most is I should have paid my fine and been on the road already, and here I am still walking the streets with my suitcase, ive been waiting to hit the road to the big cities to sell all these antiques and furniture like 7 medeaval chairs date 1550-1668 for sale now, a rare set of baker furniture bachelor chests in "yew" wood, fine arts including 1823 luigi rossini water colour, a Degas mixed media painting, and much more artworks, antiques, modern MCM lighting and collectables , among teak furniture made in denmark by skovby mobelfabrik. I have accumilated a lot over the years , all this needs to be sold now. I also sold off my stocks and the account went negative 288$, I used the money to invest in coins, the 288$ and some dollars I was planning to pay back to TD Ameritrade when my coins were sold, now im getting debt collection notices like I really needed the extra pressure.

<u>**My nickel:**</u>
as I was searching for nickels and studying the most valuable ones, I searched hundreds of nickels looking for the 1953-S and 1954-S and 60-D, 62-D 61-P, 61-D, 64-P, 63-D etc etc etc, but the mid 50s with full steps are most desirable [jefferson], so I found a beautiful 1956-P nickel and bought it and it arrived from the ebay seller and I was very happy with it, or I would have returned it, it was advertised with BU [brilliant uncirculated], condition with FS>full steps.
I included the nickel with 4 other coins knowing the nickel would be worth at least 2500-3500 **minimum**, because of my knowladge and studies of learning coins. I learn from all sources from very experienced collectors and other sources of fact, so I claimed the nickel of 3000$ value on PCGS form as a minimum because it has not been graded and I cannot determine value until the grade is on the coin. After I received back *their* junk nickel that <u>was not</u> mine, I did a very detailed research and found one comparable but not as good as mine. One sold at heritage auction for $9200 was a MS67 >1956-P with FS designation, and it looked a little cleaner than mine, but mine had a better strike, and mine had a better lustre, ill show pics to the jury, when you see all the details in the center of george washington's hair and details of the montecello building is a strong strike, the one that sold for $9200 did not have detailed hair, and kinda weak details on the monticello building, then I figure what if my nickel was a MS67+ up to a MS68 or better ?,, [MS70 is perfect]
guess we'll never know, these grades would double and triple the premium per step in grade. i.e. MS67 = 9200, MS67+ would be 15,000-18,000. MS68 would be 35,000. MS68+ would be 60,000 or more, MS69 up to MS70 you wouldnt believe it !! this approx how the charts work on pricing,

<u>**My 1964-D washington quarter:**</u>

I received back my quarters in order # 21572485 among the nickel, I looked at the 1964-D quarter that was graded a MS65 and was even dissapointed as it was undergraded and I knew it, this isnt rocket science folks, when compared to other sold quarters as now I have to show evidence in the matter, my quarter should have received a MS67 or higher grade, see discovery for pictorial evidence and reference from heritage auctions listing # 5789, theres plenty of 1964-D washington quarters with sold prices. ANOTHER 1964-D [sold at heritage], Lot # 3679 sold for 3055.00 graded a MS67+ has good strike, BUT,,,,,,, has black marks on the surface and minor scratches and die cracks on the rim also, the planchette has a spot on it and theres marks looks like paintbrush marks on the entire 'fields' of the coin like it was buffed with a cloth, or some other abrasive method leaving marks, and theres hardly no cartwheel lustre and this coin gets a MS67+ ???? theres just SSSOOOO MUCH INCONSISTANCY AND FRAUD EVERYWHERE I LOOK !!!

https://coins.ha.com/itm/washington-quarters/quarters-and-twenty-cents/1964-d-25c-ms67-pcgs-ex-coin-guy-collection-a-slender-band-of-honey-gold-patina-hugs-the-lower-obverse-border-of-this-ot/a/344-5789.s?ic4=GalleryView-Thumbnail-071515

One example of a 1964-D quarter sold for 2472.50 at heritage auctions, it has no detail in the hair and looks like a "slider" [smooth slick surface] lacking strike quality, it has a minor toning on the rim and minimal cartwheel lustre, and was graded a MS67, ?? my quarter has a much better strike, more detail, better original luster and better toned and they grade it a MS65??? [my quarter did not have any die cracks on the rim either, no wash stains, no carbon spots on the planchette EITHER!!],

So my quarter graded at a MS65 I just didnt give a dam anymore, I put it in an auction and it sold for 15$, great collections auction did not put it in their regular auction with all the population of bidders[sun-sun] they put it in some other auction and it bombed out, doesnt matter anymore, Im even getting tired of gathering all the evidence for this complaint, proving people wrong that think they can get away with whatever they want. The amount of theft & fraudulent graded coins is STAGGERING by PCGS, and they will continue to do so until arrests are made and jail-time is served. But good luck.!!!! As carnival cruise lines dumps their sewage and garbage in the ocean year after year, they just pay a 20 million dollar fine and just keep doing it. It's normal business to pay off the judges and lawyers.

let the games begin,,

Complaint #2

Order # 21569231 submission #5807343 mailed in on Feb 27th , PCGS received on march 1st, Declared value was 27,000. Submission included one 1943-P washington quarter BU, DDO (uncirculated), and one 1943-D steel lincoln cent RPM BU, with a very light green/pinkishpastel tone. Both very desirable and valuable coins. This was my first submission and PCGS did receive them on march 1st but did not post it on my member account till march 13th. It wasn't a good sign. I figured what the hell is wrong with these people claiming to be the best ??? why the delay?? Then I noticed my 1943 washington quarter that was a DDO, they had it listed as a 1942 ?!! this was now troubling me and I became very suspicious.
It's quite upsetting that these experts now have a 1942 quarter in MS60 condition worth 7$ mixed up with my 1943 DDO quarter worth 12,000 in MS60 condition. And goes up to 40,000 for MS67 !! None have been found yet in higher grades, and IT TOOK ME MANY MANY MANY HOURS TO FIND THIS ONE. MONTHS !!.So I figured mine was wort 12,500 minimum because it had no contact marks, no die cracks, the rim was also problem free, it had a strong strike and original luster, and

had a chance of seeing a high grade, **I WAS VERY UPSET** and contacted PCGS when I thought they lost it?? switched it?? or something ???? who knows what they did?? they claimed it was a typo ? These professionals making simple typo errors ? Now I was beginning to wonder. I had to call them twice and complain about the error between march 13th-15th and the error was finally fixed on monday march 18th. and what if I didnt complain about it and bring it to their attention? WHAT IF? So now im already correcting these professionals. I had so much faith in them. Not any more. I received a phone call on the march 13 from stephanie Zamarripa asking me for an extra 14$, I did not question why because I was just thinking when I sell these coins and being back on the road with my life back,,,,,,,,, I just agreed to pay whatever, figuring it was a math mistake or something I missed, welp as time passed I see that this whole fiasco was a fraud, there was no math mistake by me, no declined transaction or any evidence of ANY TRANSACTION has been found or proven, there was plenty of $$$ in the active account and the correct information was given. So why the phone call and this email? I'll get to that, this is the 13th of march and they received the 2 coins on the 1st by the way, and this is an express service [5 days] I paid for !!! the coins should have been graded and sent back already !!! so another week or so passes and I wait. Meanwhile im going back and forth with mr David Rosenberg about my other order,,,,,, I questioned mr Rosenberg more than twice about the delay on my first order, He said it was because of the 14$ being declined,,,,,,,,,,,, when I asked what was the reason for the 14$ extra charge he could not answer, when I asked to show evidence of a declined transaction,,,, he could not answer that either. Finally he responded he had no reason why there was a delay, He then said the 2 coins were going to be graded right away, then the next day he said he wasn't going to grade the 2 coins and send them back raw. I received the 2 coins back approx 28th of march, this is breech of contract among other things which ill get to in my conclusion, below is mr Rosenberg statement from march 28th email. As I have said, there never was any transaction, or declined transaction, there is NO evidence of niether, I received back my 2 coins ungraded and this was a giant dissapointment because these coins were supposed to be sold so I could get my life back in order, bla bla bla, I wrote it in the previous complaint #1

mr Rosenberg's statement

-----Original Message-----
From: David Rosenberg <DRosenberg@collectors.com>
To: antiquefineartt@aol.com <antiquefineartt@aol.com>
Cc: Joseph Pielago <JPielago@collectors.com>
Sent: Wed, Mar 27, 2019 3:16 pm
Subject: Fw: EVIDENCE FROM TROY SUMAL

"Also - with regard to your credit card declining, I cannot offer an explanation for why that happened, and I've asked the Accounting team to try again. "

email received below and my response:
Yes, thank you, and the 3 digit code is 484 on my debit card
kind regards

-----Original Message-----

From: Alma (Stephanie) Zamarripa <AZamarripa@collectors.com>
To: antiquefineartt@aol.com <antiquefineartt@aol.com>
Sent: Wed, Mar 13, 2019 2:37 pm
Subject: PLEASE READ AND REPLY: PCGS Order 21569231/Submission 5807343
Good Afternoon,

Per our conversation for submission 5807343 we will be charging $14.05 to CC-5648.

We will also be declaring the value at $13,500 each coin.

Please respond to this email authorizing the charge and changes.

Thank you,

Stephanie Zamarripa

PCGS Problem Order Specialist

p 800.447.8848 | f 949.567.1253

PCGS.com

__THE DEBIT CHARGE CHARADE:__ [an act or event that is clearly false]
I would like mr Rosenberg and ms Zamarripa explain to the jury and your Honor this 3 week delay of
my first order of which a reason was fabricated of a "declined" transaction, then **why** wasnt I called
when the transaction was alledgedly declined? What kind of a person would claim to charge me 14$
without giving reason and then follow up with email for my authorization, and then not charge the 14$,,
AND THEN at a later time say it was declined??? the transaction wasnt declined either,,, it never
happend. There's no record OF ANY TRANSACTION WHATSOEVER. And mr Rosenberg used this
for a reason to delay my two coins when the actual reason i think he was stalling for time while looking
for two similar coins to swap out for my 2 rare coins !
With the amount of numerous mistakes & shenannigans, anybody would think the same thing. I
provided an email with my account ending in 5648 showing funds available and an active account for
that month, and I had no answer to any questions of this particular charade, see email records in
discovery. [mr Rosenberg said he had no answer to the question]

The fact of the matter is that there was NEVER any transaction ! Declined or otherwise, theres no
proof of anything, and mr Rosenberg stated to me "he doesnt know why the delay" well heres my
answer; **mr Rosenberg and/or his associate[s] whoever it may be WAS LOOKING FOR COINS
THAT LOOKED SIMILAR TO MY VALUABLE 1943 DDO QUARTER AND 1943 D/D STEEL
PENNY BECAUSE THEY WERE GOING TO SWAP THEM OUT AND STEAL THEM
ALSO,!!!!!!!! these coins are not readily available and if I hadnt complained and called them who
knows what might have happened !!!** I think a jury would conclude the same thing too,
I have not received **ANY** "professional service" or "expertise" from PCGS/ Collectors Universe, as the
facts show, and I did ask that question numerous times, and nobody answered me. The email
communication with mr Rosenberg and his attorney mr Kieth Attlesey show lying and fraud, there is
also history [I seen online] of the CEO [Joe Orlando] of collectors universe of lying on the stand under
oath, This company has quite a record of dishonesty, as I am going to print out as much as I can for

evidence. Mr Kieth Attlesey was sent an affidavit from me and he did receive it on the 19th of April, he had 14 business days to respond or he has acquiesced, that time has now expired.

CONCLUSION

I can only think and believe now PCGS/Collectors Universe is a criminal, they talk like criminals and they act like criminals, They will steal and commit fraud as much as they think they can get away with !! I tried to resolve this case and get back my property they have taken from me, I am told that is hostile and abusive and harrassing? Even their attorney I have caught in lies as well as David Rosenberg caught in lies, and now the stephanie woman is tied up in this conglomerate of lies and frauds with this fictitious "declined transaction" that never happened. I surely think they were going to switch out my two other coins if I had not stepped up and said something and complained about it.

After my experience[s] research of PCGS/Collectors Universe, I may determine that first time coin applicants and members are targeted, as I see similar complaints online mostly from first time submissions and a pattern of no communication and stubborness from V.P. Director David Rosenberg, one complaintant said that the attny Kieth Attlesey even refused to speak. My 1956-P Jefferson nickel was swapped [stolen], it had full steps and was a high grade coin, the rest of the order was botched up, my other two coins on a seperate submission were not easily that replacable is why they delayed the order so long WITHOUT A VALID REASON !!! you cant just find a 1943 DDO washington quarter in a mint state condition or a 1943 D/D steel cent, these are rare and valuable, and my thoughts tell me that they **were looking for coins to switch them also**. like I said earlier WHAT IF I DIDNT COMPLAIN ?? and stay on them with making phone calls?? PCGS/Collectors Universe used somebodys name falsley on over 14,000 COAs and had to settle 10.5 million to the plaintiff. And also thier CEO [Joe Orlando] lies under oath on the stand, [I read in one case], lots more on this company as I have to spend my time now to show how dirty they are, I'd like to know how they make a decision to profile somebody and steal from them, thinking they will get away with another theft of fraud, mr Rosenberg seems to be in control of the accounting and customer service and whatever else, he tells them what to do and what to say and they listen wether its right or wrong.

** http://www.net54baseball.com/showthread.php?t=79113

"The jury found that Collectors Universe used Miller's name on 14,060 Certificates of Authenticity without his permission."

Examples of complaints below of other frauds and stealing found on BBB, YELP, pissedcustomer.com:

*12/21/2018

On Nov.15, 2018 i submitted a packet to PCGS for coin grading services. Days later, the company submitted a photo of coin: 1058 Franklin Half dollar appeared on my member web page. This was not my coin. After talking to a PCGS representive they said my coin. To resolve the matter, I asked to inspaect the photos and videos of the examination process concerning coin only. This was denied. They also stated they are refusing my FOIA request. The company has misplace my coin.

02/17/2017

** I sent in a 1964 special Kennedy half dollar (rare) I got this from my father as a old set along with many high grade coins. I sent it in and received a coin as thought a 1964 sp Kennedy graded MS68 which I thought low in comparing to their coins. I had taken pictures before sending and comparisons to other same year coins. I received my coin and first thought all good, then tried to leverage my coin for a small loan and found out the numbers on the coin did not match the coin on their site. It came up as a 1964 proof worth 67.00 This is a 50k dollar coin and after researching what I was told I was furious but then... I noticed a flaw in the label and to my surprise I peeled off the sp68 label to find another label underneath! I was shocked and I do not believe I have the same coin I sent in. I know it doess not compare side by side as a proof or mint set 1964 Kennedy. I believe it was switched and someone put a phoney sticker over it after I had called to request they make sure to examine this rare coin thoroughly. I also noticed that the papers they sent back were check off as the grade the right coin and value I had stated but this paper did not have my signature or date as required by their company and I know for fact I signed all copies. I have tried contacting them and customer service people were very rude to me about my complaint. I will not only demand all my fees and membership fees back but if I do not get "my coin" back it will then escalate.

*** PCGS coin grading service //Collectors Universe // David Rosenberg Stole a rare coin, replaced with other, relabeled holder fake label not the 47k coin i sent value of coin returned $61.00 Newport Beach, CA Internet // Cal.// Illinois

I had joined PCGS coingrading service to have my high end and some rare coins graded handed down by my father.

I had researched for weeks before paying a $149.00 membership fee as worried on losing my $47,000 coin for grading as i read BBB had some simalar reports.

Idid it as i thought ok, its safe nothing bad will happen.

I sent my rare coin after taking pictures and comparisons to other coins that look the same but not rare as this one particcular coin.

I paid a grading fee of $192.00 and my shipping of $32.00 with insurance.

I finally received my coin much later than paid for and it had the label and what i expected a 1964 SP GRADE 68

I was using it as collateral for a small loan but the lender said the numbers on the coin label did not match PCGS web site for that coin.

I called them and after researching this my self with no response from the company i eventually found the label on the front of coin holder was crooked so a peeled it back a little to see another label underneath, inside the holder stating a different coin as worth $61. [continued below]....

....00

SOMEONE HAD SWAPPED MY COIN AND SENT A DIFFERENT COIN BUT DID NOT CHANGE THE LABEL ONLY TO ADD A LABEL OVER THE TOP OF THE HOLDER.

I had tried to work with the company V.P. David Rosenberg but he referred me to their atty and then tried sending me a $21.00 check after requesting cancellation of membership ($149.00) and my coin. nothing was done by him, the atty or anyone. Atty Kieth Attelsey never responded to me or my calls.

I have filed complaint with BBB, State of Cal. Atty general and State atty general in South Dakota where i live.

I am now going to pursue major legal action as i have the proof of my real coin, their coin not the same and a video and pictures of the fake label placed over the holder.

I want my refunds of over $350.00 and i want my coin or at least a replacment of equal value!!

I would never send coins to this company read the BBB reports and research them before wanting to do busness.

David C. Hicks

This report was posted on **Ripoff Report** on 03/09/2017 12:04 PM and is a permanent record located here: https://www.ripoffreport.com/reports/pcgs-coin-grading-service/internet/pcgs-coin-grading-service-collectors-universe-david-rosenberg-stole-a-rare-coin-re-1360764. The posting time indicated is Arizona local time. Arizona does not observe daylight savings so the post time may be Mountain or Pacific depending on the time of year. Ripoff Report has an exclusive license to this report. It may not be copied without the written permission of Ripoff Report. READ: Foreign websites steal our content

******** I following process I follow protocol I'm dealing with the company right now I'm complaining about my billing I'm complaining about my service I'm complaining about my order getting changed without authorization on two separate orders I'm complaining about coin switched that were valuable. At this point my graded coins we're all undergraded and categorize with everyone else. So they can control value I'm complaining zero customer service from day one December 2018 an incomplete packet. On a gold membership at $149 no submission forms. My valuable coins were switched out. Post office tells me my order picked up. 6 days later PCGS tells me it arrives. thus a lot of time for switching Out of a total of 28 coins 18 were switched they must think I'm really green took a lot of pictures. Not done... No Stars negative. Read less

********* I joined on December 14, 2018. Same day decided to cancel membership. I have phoned four times since, still no credit to my account for cancelling membership. Each phone call I am assured it will be processed in a week.

****** I sent Pcgs a cc double eagle. This coin was slabbed by a company known for way over grading their coins. Pcgs would not grade the coin because it was "cleaned". Doubting that the coin was cleaned I took the coin removed the slab and sent it back to pcgs. This time the coin came back ms60. I don't think I will do business with them again.

******* I got PCGS membership to try and see firsthand about their grading process. I had 4 NGC slabbed gold eagles, which looked pristine and I've examined under 5x & 10x prior sending.

My first complaint, I used 4 free complimentary vouchers but the PCGS costumer rep tried to charge me for expedited service at $60 a coin without my permission to do it. When called to have it changed back, I had to speak to 3 agents to get the issue resolved and the 1st agent refused to help me flat out and said there is nothing they can do to change it back!

My second complaint, none of the coins crossed to PCGS, which is very strange considering their crossing rate is about 50% around this time and I've consulted respected professional service prior submission which agrees with me. I've seen countless PCGS graded coins looking substantially worst then these pristine eagles. I've also seen large dealers in particular having PCGS graded eagles which looked worst than coins I have sent.

Third, I was away on foreign trip for few weeks and asked PCGS to hold the coins in their vault until I get back. They said it wasn't a problem and they would hold them. They did not, the coins have been shipped right after grading and have been sitting in post office for over a week. Thankfully, I was able to get back in time to claim them 1 day before they were going to be shipped back to sender.

I've been in the coin collecting and grading business for about 3 years now, and this has given me some first hand negative experience with PCGS that I've read about on various forums but I didn't believe until I tried myself.

Bottom line, I am cancelling my membership and will not send for grading to them again. I will also avoid buying PCGS graded coins from here on out, unless there is no other option available for given coin and I am able to verify the coin is true to its grade prior purchase. I think their business practices are very bad and their grading etiquette could have negative impact on coin collecting as a whole. Very disappointing experience.

******* PCGS, like many other coin grading services, has literally destroyed the numismatic industry and the joy of coin collecting. Apparently, complete morons (many with little or no education) take a short course to become coin grading 'professionals'. So, basically, you pay a premium (and, yes, they are NOT cheap) to have some one-brain-cell jerk tell you that all of your coins are worthless. I submitted a small lot of somewhat rare coins that were kept in protective, plastic cases for well over 30 years. These coins were marked as 'cleaned' and then placed into a plastic tomb that you need a sledge hammer to remove. So, now, I can't even sell these coins because they're marked as garbage by some turd-brained know-it -all. Forget these guys. Bury your coins in your backyard. Dig 'em up in 30 years, don't wash 'em, and sell 'em. However, if you're really into wasting money, then go ahead and send your coins to PCGS. AND, don't say you haven't been warned.

******* NEVER SUBMIT TO PCGS!!!! THEY LOST MY MEMBERSHIP NOW after I sent in 40 coins, 20 were proof Morgan's they sent them back to me all with business strike grades.. not even

PL on them! I sent the 20 proofs to NGC, all 20 came back proofs! Done and done! My opinion and my experience, I know very well it may not seem like it matters, but it just takes one drop to start a lake, and in my opinion, I've heard this same story of mine so many times.. and felt it wasn't real, I was going to see for myself! what a HUGE waste of thousands of dollars! Don't make the same mistake! Go NGC! I predict this company is going to slowly go under!

********* Sent them a proof Lunar coin from Australia. These coins are extremely popular and everyone knows them. Well, apparently PCGS has no idea what they are. While it came back as a 70, it was grade a MS and not a PF or proof. This completely boggled my mind as there are multiple "quality" checkpoints with numerous people confirming and verifying that the grade on the plastic is correct. REALLY?? But wait, it gets better. So I ended up sending it back to them. I explained what the coin is (not to mention I had marked it as PROOF on the submission form) and that they made a mistake. So I send it back and what does it come back as.....you guessed it, a MS coin....AGAIN! Almost fell off my chair when I saw the grade online (which took absolutely forever, literally 60 business days). At that point, I asked to cancel my membership and demanded my membership fee back and to just send my coin back to me. Sold my coin and never bought a PCGS graded coin again. In fact, I don't even collect anymore. I'm thoroughly convinced that they hire people who have ZERO interest in coins. People just looking for a paycheck, have no prior knowledge to collecting or have never collected themselves before. This company is highly overrated but don't take my word for it, just read the other 1-2 starred reviews on here

********** I joined PCGS a few weeks ago. I dealt with Jennifer in customer service. I had questions about different aspects of my membership. I also sent Jennifer pictures of a coin I wanted to get graded. She requested that I send them to her. Well that was the last time I heard from her. I tried getting some answers from some one else in customer service and was told that Jennifer would have to help me. I left two or three messages on her voice mail. She never responded back to me. I finally made contact with her via telephone. She could not tell me why she didn't respond. She sounded so disorganized and confused. Well, if that was any indication of customer service with PCGS, I wanted nothing to do with this company. "Customer service" is a contradiction in terms with PCGS. I cancelled my membership with her. She didn't even apologize or make any attempt to rectify the situation. I really think I dodged a bullet with this company. I have many coins that I need to get graded. Going to use NGC.

*********** I wish I had read these reviews before sending my coins and spending hundreds of dollars on PCGS coin grading services. As soon as I receive the rest of my coins back from them, I will be canceling my membership. Like others have mentioned, the coin grading services at PCGS are sub-par. Here's one example...I have a 1882-O/S Morgan Vam 4 that was graded as a MS64 by NGC. I had two independent, local coin dealers examine the coin and they agreed with the NGC grade. Each of these dealers have 20+ years of experience in the industry. This coin was in a NGC holder and since I'm a PCGS member I decided to send it to PCGS to get a regrade. I received the coin back as a DNC/Cleaned. If the coin doesn't grade higher than a MS64 then I understand the DNC but I don't believe at all, for one second, that this coin was cleaned. A cleaned coin, as most collectors know, reduces the coin's value. I specifically had independent dealers look at the 1882 O/S coin beforehand because I've had other coins graded by PCGS that I believe were graded well below the grade they should have been. This time I wanted to get a "second opinion" and I'm glad I did. I have no confidence in the PCGS coin grading process and I would never recommend this company to anyone

✳✳✳✳✳✳✳✳✳✳✳✳ Well, I had to call again today, but I called billing instead. They took care of me and my coins have been shipped. They were supposed to be shipped last week, however, customer service lied to me. After calling billing, a section that should not be involved, they fixed my problem in less than 10 minutes. If you deal with this business, be ready to be disappointed.

✳✳✳✳✳✳✳✳✳✳✳✳ I'm extremely disappointed in this business and their vision. There is no sense of urgency no matter what. Everything that I've read people have gotten their coins late, as I am still going through trying to get mine back. The "customer service" personnel constantly say that those are suggested times, but when it continuously happens, maybe you should update your information. I suggest you do this annually at least. I just called the "business" to inquire about my coins that were sent in regular and received on August 18th, it is now September 21st and they still have not been shipped. There was an issue with payment, I addressed it immediately September 16th and I see it still has not shipped as of today. I call customer service AGAIN and inquire about the status. After some condescending talk from the customer service woman, I ensured she understood my situation. She then became downright disrespectful and continued cutting me off during my communication portion to say she has told me 3 times that she's going to contact shipping to take the hold off of my order which was already taken off September 16th. When she cut me short, I went to ask for the woman's name and she had already hung up on me. This is a poorly run organization, their information is incorrect, I do question their grading practices and I'm extremely disappointed to have paid so much for a membership just to get substandard service and disrespected by customer service. This is honestly blowing my mind right now. I believe your customers deserve much better service from this company with your astronomical membership prices and insane coin grading fees. I would highly suggest using another coin grading service if you plan on having your coins graded. I'm thoroughly disappointed. I would like to do business with one company that has some ethics. I guess I will be doing more thorough research on the next coin grading service I use

✳✳✳✳✳✳✳✳✳✳✳✳ How can a coin with a scratch be graded as SP70 ? How can I trust PCGS ?

✳✳✳✳✳✳✳✳✳✳✳✳ Last Summer I sent in a coin due to an interior defect in the holder. PCGS did not get it back to me until 6 months later. However, that took constant calling to the representative as the status of my order. When I finally received my coin back nothing was done to the coin. They claim that there is nothing wrong with the holder when there was two obvious distortions on the reverse side of the coin. PCGS didn't even bother to open the holder to look into the matter as I left my credit card information on the order request so if it wasn't the holder than they can bill me for it. This was such a disappointment that I hesitate to purchase coins with this grading service. PCGS has NO CUSTOMER SERVICE so avoid the company if you can!!!!

✳✳✳✳✳✳✳✳✳✳✳✳ Lately, I had someone else send in a few coins for me to PCGS and guess what! ?

The cheep coins were graded appropriately and the more expensive expensive ones were graded as CLEANED!.....Hummmm?

Is it because I don't go through a coin dealer that has a financial relationship with them PCGS and cost more to go through them... and private citizens that submit their coins as individuals are beat up by the PCGS's graders. ..?

************** The treatment I received was as if I couldn't have been a SMALLER Fish!

 I was treated rudely, I was belittled for expecting--- 'Plain Ol' Customer Service'! You know! The kind of service where the Business Owner or Representative Smiles, asks you "How are you?" or "Can I help you?" --- Not ---- Stand up in front of you, looking down at you like you are a flea, and addressing you as if you are bothering or taking up their time. I have since left PCGS for LIFE!---OUT

Easily the worst coin grading service out there on several levels, and with a rude, arrogant, and incompetent customer service dept. to go along.

My review would mirror Steve M. Wish I could give ZERO stars.

**********************This is the 'go to' company if you require non existent customer service, your coins returned damaged, and the grading consistency of a casino roulette wheel. Actually hard to believe a company like this is even still in business. The only thing they seem to be quite proficient at is continually coming up with new schemes and gimmicks to get people to keep re-sending in the same old coins over and over**

I 'm also in agreement with Steve M. and Victor H.

I went to Long Beach coin show for the past three to four year. There is no customer service, I was gotta join PCGS a few year back. but after talking to them, the way they address to you, as V. H mention, like you are a flea. I since then I went to join with NGC.

Now after all these year, I went to the Long Beach Coin show and talked to PCGS, I decided to continues with NGC.

My notes on toning fraud:
On the title below found on a website I have pic [1 of many], of fake toned coins of which PCGS has graded, falsley graded coins and fraudulent coins all graded by PCGS, they do whatever they want because there is no authority to stop them, thay laugh at the consumer[s] and continue the frauds, see pics of evidence in my discovery, I could make a career of tracking down these fraudulent graded coins theres so many I'm finding without much effort because I am researching coin toning because of their "opinion" they said my quarters were "questionable color" and "ungradable" when on the contrary PCGS is grading coins that are obvious fakes !!!

Fake Rainbow COIN TALK Toned Coins - Artificial Colors | Coin Talk

<u>CLAIM FOR RELIEF</u>

1. <u>Plaintiff declaratory relief, compensatory damages, punitive damages, liquidated damages, and reasonable attorneys' fees and costs as remedies for Plaintiff's' financial losses and extreme duress & mental anguish</u>

Damages:

Theft of my 1956-P jefferson nickel estimated value	$10,000-18,000
breech of contract on order # 21569231	7500.00
multiple frauds including lying	4500.00
emotional duress mental anguish	

defamation of my property>false labels and words on my 3 washington quarters & prevention of sale. the alledged value of all three quarters minimum value

> >>   17,000.00

one 1964-D washington quarter undergraded

fair market value 2400-3000   2400.00

one is in discovery, the other two are being researched and possibly being sent off to a lab for REAL PROFESSIONAL service

restriction on my advancement in life 2 ½ to 4 ½ months delay because I have to start all over again !!   15,000.00

legal fees over 47 hours, maybe 60 hours   12,500.00

punative >>>   85,000.00

<u>Total</u> _______________________________________ $ 158,900.00

The Undersigned, I, troy sumal, do herewith declare, state and say that I, troy sumal with sincere intent in truth, that I, the undersigned am competent by stating the matters set forth herein, that the contents are true, correct, complete, and certain, admissible as evidence, reasonable, not misleading, and by My best knowledge, by Me, the undersigned.

CLERK'S DETERMINATION

Based on the information in this Application, I have determined the applicant to be ( ) Indigent ( ) Not Indigent, according to s. 57.082, F.S.

Dated this __________ day of _______________, 20 _____.

Clerk of the Circuit Court by ______________________

This form was completed with the assistance of: ______________________________________

Clerk/Deputy Clerk/Other authorized person.

APPLICANTS FOUND NOT TO BE INDIGENT MAY SEEK REVIEW BY A JUDGE BY ASKING FOR A HEARING TIME. THERE IS NO FEE FOR THIS REVIEW.

Sign here if you want the judge to review the clerk's decision ______________________________________

I met a woman named Lily, I've been talking to since June of 2017, during the passing of time she became interested in coin collecting and was studying coins with me and seeing the beautiful coins that I have in my collection. I was showing her by emailing pictures, and I began teaching her. (lily bought some beautiful coins from ebay also from my advisement, but now doesnt want to have any graded because of what I experienced), Seeing how I didnt have a life anyways since the creeps took my driver license for the purposes of extortion (I wrote a book on that also), so anyways I spent all my time on studying coins, even woke up in the middle of the night and studied on my phone. I know the best videos on youtube & other sources of which Im not going to name because of liability, so anyways my eyes were very well trained and getting better all the time. Over the past years I had just bought coins casually at the flea market and from private sellers I met on craigslist and offer up. I didnt get serious about buying until 2018,,,,,,,well thats when the money came in for me when I sold my teak furniture made in denmark. In Dec 2018 a man contacted me from davie FL, he claimed to have quite a lot of coins he wanted to get rid of. I was very excited. Althoiugh the address was located where the buses didnt run, I called lily to help me with uber,, I didnt know anything about uber so she arranged for the driver to take me from the closest bus stop then pick me up when I was ready to leave, I had my big suitcase with me made by Tumi, Well I spent over 2 hours looking at coins and there was quite a load, the man let me pick through everything and choose what I wanted. By the time we negotiated the price it was around 375-400 $ and my suitcase weighed well over 100 pounds. The uber driver had to help me lift it into the trunk of the car, and took me to the bus stop, On the way back all buses had to lower the handicap ramp for me to get it on and off the bus. At this time the coin collecting became serious, because of more research and more purchases made in the following year, and I sold some of them but not much, I still have most of them. Blue whitman folders full of mercury dimes, jefferson nickels, indian head cents, lincoln cents, over 60 blue folders, and mostly modern U.S. Coins, some uncirculated. Many BU rolls and many in dealer envelopes from the 1970's and many loose coins, and a lot in plastic flips, a very wide variety, I showed lily the pics and she was so happy for me.

 And it took me months to go through these coins and sort through them and place them into my notebook binnders, over the next couple of years I kept showing her my coins and telling her my plans of what I would like to do to get a house to live in so I wouldn't have to stay in my truck anymore. After my 8 years of research of coins and building up a nice collection it was time to start selling them, me and Lily agreed I had some really beautiful ones because I was showing her what was selling at the auction and we were comparing them to what I have and definitely I had some super nice examples ms67s and some nice varieties and mint errors. Lily has come to know me as a very persistent researcher and only dealing with the facts as in the past I took care of all her debts with my knowledge of credit score repair, I wiped out over 65,000 worth of debts in three and a half weeks,,, not bragging but that's just a reference of how quickly I can retain information and learn the facts,.. so it came a time in Feb 2019 I picked out some really beautiful coins from my collection, some of my best to send into PCGS. I didn't even have the money at the time so Lily lent me the money I think it was a little bit over $400 for two submissions. We both were so confident I would sell these coins for $25 to $30,000 because comparing to what has been sold at the auctions evidence was clear what I had. Then I could pay Lily back and get a trailer and move all my stuff into a house and deal with the rest of this collection. But evidently this **turned into one gigantic nightmare** that I will never forget and still to this day this has put a great strain on me. This day It's still a nightmare as I think back when I was showing everybody the comparison pictures of my original nickel I sent to PCGS and the nickel they sent back to me and everyone saying its not the same nickel, they switched it. Lily is still very upset to this day because of all the setbacks this has done to me. But yet with the blatent evidence not one lawyer will take the case. Yeah it's a nightmare alright. And I'm sure there are many other people who have sent in their best coins to PCGS hoping to get a Fair treatment from these "best rated professionals", but in returned got FUCKED.

I found the picture of my 1964 washington quarter (pic next page),
that was undergraded by PCGS, by comparison looking at sold examples this should have been graded MS67-67+. Its heartwrenching to see my beautiful quarter defiled by crooks,
 UGH !!!!!!! 2000-4000 quarter now worth 15$$!!!! NGC is doing the same thing !! Another book coming !

1964-D 25C

PCGS MS65

5877.65/37904680

The secrecy,

 what I don't understand is this; if this coin grading service is claiming to be so professional, then why is there no employee roster and why is nobody allowed to speak with any coin grader ?? And why is no video available to be seen of the customers coins when the customer knows that their coin has been stolen?? Even the police and all government offices have an employee roster. Auction houses have employee disclosure also.

So what is PCGS hiding?? . I sent in a few coins to ICG recently , and you know what they were nice enough to give me a call, one of their primary coin graders by the name of skip called my number and left me a message to discuss a coin I sent to them with environmental damage, and he spoke freely to me about my other coins one of them had a wheel mark on it. I thought this was mostly professional and courteous of this coin grader. He even mentioned to me the name of the advanced grader I forget what he called it. "Master examiner" ? This is how professionals should be. even though ICG doesn't have the best reputation, (because of PCGS running them down with their propaganda), I don't know what to say about that all I'm saying is they were very transparent and they did call the customer (me).

 As I have sent in coins recently now to NGC, I'm finding that they have common practices as PCGS. VERY SECRETIVE. AND EXTREMELY FRAUDULENT !! I can't wait to start writing what they did to me. And it's all facts nothing is speculation. They are the second biggest criminal in The coin grading industry. I am not the type to allow people to SCREW ME and do nothing about it. If I do not complain that means it is implied consent. So I strongly advise everybody to be complaining and exposing the crimes and fraud of PCGS & NGC.

I wonder what is the source of all the propaganda that PCGS is the best coin grader? How many millions do they spend paying journalists and for advertising?? And why do the auction houses use them continuously without investigating their criminal history ?? Why all the hype ? Is anybody awake and capable of critical thinking to see this pattern of theft ? And it surely will continue because it is a pattern. The collectors and dealers who have been burnt have to smarten up and find a way to stop them. Speak up more and keep complaining !! publish books, make videos, use social media, get friends to help. GETTUM !!!